D1642051

THANK GOD FOR WOMEN PREACHERS

Benjamin Blankenship

Contents:

ACKNOWLEDGEMENTS

The Holy Spirit spoke to my heart guiding me to write this book, and a fair deal of work went into it. I'm thankful for my family and church family for enduring all of the long hours of studying which I'd taken in preparing this book.

Likewise, I'd like to thank all of my proof readers. My wife, Victoria Blankenship, like myself she is heavily involved in music, ministry, and healing those who are hurting. She is an accomplished singer/songwriter and pianist. I call her Queen Victoria. She's everything I've ever prayed for in a wife. She's my partner working along side me as a perfect equal. In many regards the differences in her personality keep my eccentric avant-garde nature tethered a bit closer to what is socially acceptable amidst our peers.

Thank God for Women Preacher's second editor was my co-worker Victoria Klouda. She is a University of

Tennessee graduate, with a lengthy background in the swimming industry. Additionally, Victoria loves to read and write. She's extraordinarily proficient, and works quickly. Frankly, it came as a pleasant surprise when she offered to come aboard as an editor.

Finally, the third editor was Letty Plantz. She went thoroughly went over the book just to make certain everything was silky smooth. Letty writes, sings, and plays keyboard for the band Jesus Phreak Blues. She and her husband James are terrific people, and musically I could listen to them all day long and never get board. They're both really fantastic.

I'm thankful for Rev. Dale and Trish Harvey. They came down to Benchmark Church, 961 East Tri-County Boulevard, Oliver Springs, Tennessee each Friday night for the several months that I was writing this book. Dale would preach in my stead which allowed me the extra time I needed to write and prepare each chapter.

Every time before writing I'd pray heavily, as I knew then that someone somewhere will look to criticize every statement made within these pages. Our congregation has been praying. We continue to pray that this book will minister to those that are oppressed or suppressed wrongfully. My goal isn't to make someone change their mind. I really feel like we all have a final authority. For cultist like Jim Jones, it's themselves. Historically, Jim Jones admittedly wasn't a Christian, but a socialist who saw himself as God. He'd quote or misquote the Bible, giving it a nod, and then continue to drone on for hours with his socialistic propaganda. He hunted for ignorant, illiterate people who didn't know what the truth looked like, so they could be lead captive by his lies.

I'm thankful for everyone who is genuinely reading this objectively. It's my deep hope that this book, "Thank God For Women Preachers" helps someone, somewhere, somehow. Thank you in advance for reading.

INTRODUCTION

Sometime ago during one of Benchmark Church's Friday night services, where I pastor, we began a by request series. On one given night I taught on the subject of "Women In Ministry", which actually had rabbit-trailed off of another subject. Buzzing through ten pages of notes, and watching the clock out of the corner of my eye, I hopscotched through the notes finishing in about one hours time. The message was posted on Youtube and Facebook.

Several people approached me regarding this. One man from the annals of cyberspace called me a feminist, several misogynists didn't like it, but what stands out in my mind is the one woman who with tear-filled eye told me that she never thought God would call a woman into ministry. She added that she'd been raised Baptist and that's what she'd always been told. She thanked me for showing her through the Bible that everything they preached in relation to that was wrong.

A little while passed by and I felt the Holy Spirit leading me to write a book on the subject. It was something that I wrestled with a little bit. Honestly, I just wanted to be absolutely certain that it wasn't just me thinking it. After all, I've been raised in church my whole life and can say with certainty that there are an abundance of spiritually ignorant men in ministry, and laity in the pews who may dislike it. I also know that due to poor hermeneutics coupled with a few other issues what should be a peaceful Bible discussion, can turn into a heated battle. While I touch on that a bit, the huge question that could be asked is, "Why, would someone who says they believe the whole Bible is the inspired world of God get upset when you layout the whole Bible to put scripture into context as the writers and readers of that time period would have understood it?"

This book was written with some level of personal tension, as I know some sanctimonious people will hate me for writing it. That too is a bit disturbing, seeing how as Christians there are issues we should be able to disagree on and still love each other. My sincere hope is that people can read this with an open mind. If you're 100% for women within ministry you should have sound Biblical reasoning to back it up and this book will give it to you. If you are not in favor of women in ministry, you should be open to the possibility that you may be wrong. After all seeing as how none of us are God, it'd be irrational not to think that we're wrong about something.

Beyond the subject of women in ministry, there is also a chapter on divorcees in ministry, which analyzes what scripture says in relation to divorcees. That scripture goes in-depth with the qualifications of deacons and bishops. It also expounds on what the Bible says in regards to divorce.

The truth is that if you're a teacher or preacher; someone in church leadership, God is going to hold you to a higher standard. No matter how you look at any of these issues a big question is are you, the person in leadership being a good Christian example. I hope this book blesses you and is an enjoyable, easy read.

Pastor Benjamin Blankenship

CHAPTER 1:
WHAT IN THE WORD?

Years ago, when I was a minister in my early twenties; I'd stopped in to visit an area church that had a woman who served as it's pastor. She was very well spoken, and for that matter came off as quite fiery as well. As their church's Sunday School began she went back into some of the classrooms to teach while the adult class was taught by her husband. It was my first time stopping in for a morning service there, and thereby my first time in one of their Sunday school classes as well.

On that particular morning, a family who had once attended another church, which I also had formerly attended, came in to visit as well. Recognizing me, the man spoke chipperly. It was a short conversation and then the lesson went underway.

Have you ever been in a situation that is so insane that it's like a crazy dream? I have, and this class was going to be one of those times. It ranked up there with the time that a mother was picking lice out of her daughter's hair and flipping them across the sanctuary of a little backwoods church while I preached. Seemingly just as quick as it began, that day's adult Sunday school lesson was about to go off the rails.

The topic was on pornography- or if it wasn't, then it turned into a conversation about pornography. The pastor's husband began to explain in intricate depth how Playboy magazine is different in different parts of the world. He explained that in Muslim countries they couldn't show the female form in the nude, but rather in scantily clad boudoir type imagery. As he continued his vivid and robust monolog on the expansive cornucopia of types of pornography there are, the visiting man who had greeted me was much more than happy to chime in.

This monolog had become a conversation, and from there had quickly evolved into a challenge as to who knew the most about the pornographic industry from their own wealth of personal experience. Shocking as it was, this Sunday School classroom became a platform for who had viewed more porn. I recall that one of the men was exclaiming that he'd seen so much porn it could fill and entire dumpster, while the other retorted that he'd seen so much pornography that it could not only fill a dumpster, but overflow it and go to spilling out into the street. The entire matter was wildly inappropriate to say the least.

These weren't shame filled admissions of regret. There was no remorse, regret, or repentance that was spoken of. The sanctuary of that small church had been reduced to the equivalent of a smut filled middle school boys locker room. I sat there quietly astounded by the Godless stupidity that had spun out of control. The class ended with not so much as a prayer being said.

The church's classrooms began to empty out into the sanctuary. Seemingly, some sense of sanity would overtake the remainder of the church service at this point. As people began to congregate together, the pastor's husband stepped off of the pulpit and took a seat. Amongst the shuffling around in that moment it almost feels like there was a silence that filled the air.

The visiting man, who'd previously acted the fool in class, asked me nervously where the man went who was teaching. I told him that he's sitting over there. People were still moving around as his eyes were scouting over the crowd. He then asked me where a certain preacher was; asking for him by name. I replied, "He hasn't been here in about 5 years". The lady pastor stepped up onto the pulpit and began speaking. To be honest, I don't remember a thing she said. That visitor was still talking in my ear.

He inquired, "Who is she?" I answered, "She's the pastor." With a look that he couldn't hide, and presumably wouldn't hide if he could; this admitted porn addict, hypocrite, and braggart, proceeded to act slightly more asinine than he had during the previous thirty minutes. He belted out loudly, "Well, I don't believe in that!" Repeating, just to be certain that everyone knew how strong his misappropriated convictions were, "I don't believe in women preachers."

From that point he boisterously exclaimed to his wife and children, "C'mon, We're leaving!" With a look of embarrassment on her face his wife gathered their children and made a clamorous departure from the church.

For moments that felt like they were held in suspension in time, awkwardness lingered in the air from how this ignorant man acted publicly in that little church. With that said, the thought of women teaching men, preaching to men, being in authority over men, or speaking in church in any regard is a topic that quite a lot of people still take an issue with.

Today in the twenty first century we're living in an era where extraordinary amounts of information are just a click away, and yet so many people are so far from understanding what the Bible says about any given subject. We're in a generation where theologians have become a thing of the past. It seems in this age that most parishioners across the United States typically sit in their church's comfortable seating with their cellphones left on, volume left on, listen to or endure the music, listen to or endure a twenty-five to forty-five-minute sermon once a week, if that. Then they go home, and turn on the television without a second thought.

Yet the message is preached again and again that in regard to ministry, women just need to shut up. The tragedy is that it scripture is being mutilated. Scripture is not contextualized and subsequently it's being misquoted over and over again.

Perhaps it's time we began to ask ourselves, "What does the Bible actually teach regarding women in ministry? Is anything lost in the English translation? If the Bible doesn't contradict itself, then why do we see repetitive evidence of women in God ordained ministry within scripture? What ministerial roles do we find women in within scripture? What was specifically going on in Ephesus, where Timothy ministered? What was the situation pertaining to the passage of scripture regarding women that was written to the church in Corinth?"

Women in ministry is a widely taught subject, and if you're in opposition to it, your understanding is wrong. It's time we got back to what the Bible actually teaches, instead of leaning on the blind guidance of unlearned, unstudied, unprepared, insecure men. It's time for real Christians to stand up and actively follow Christ, refusing to swallow every thing that you're fed. Ask questions, study adamantly like the Bereans.

The Apostle Paul's Letter to Timothy at the Church in Ephesus

Within the Bible there are several passages of scripture that people equate to standing against women being called into ministry. One of those places is found within the second chapter of 1st Timothy. It read:

"In like manner also, that women adorn themselves in modest apparel, with shamefacedness and sobriety; not with braided hair, or gold, or pearls, or costly array; But (which becometh women professing godliness) with good works. Let the woman learn in silence with all subjection. But I suffer not a woman to teach, nor to usurp authority over the man, but to be in silence. For Adam was first formed, then Eve. And Adam was not deceived, but the woman being deceived was in the transgression. Notwithstanding she shall be saved in childbearing, if they continue in faith and charity and holiness with sobriety." (1st Timothy 2:9-15, KJV)

Understandably, 1st Timothy was a letter from Paul to this young pastor who is regarded as his son in the faith. Just as Moses was a spiritual father and mentor to Joshua, and Elijah was a spiritual mentor and father to Elisha, Paul was all of those things to this young Pastor. Timothy pastored in the huge city of Ephesus. It was a city that Paul had a burden for. He lived there for four years. Many notable accounts happened there throughout history and within the New Testament itself.

As any letter written an observant reader would expect there to be a perpetual trail of bread crumbs expounding on what was going on there in that time and in that place. While someone who is not a student of the Bible and history might otherwise miss those nuances, I will try to make a point to highlight them within the confines of this book.

One question that people frequently ask regarding passages of scripture like this is, "Were these instructions regarding a certain place or situation, or is this all-inclusive?" It's certainly a legitimate question, when you consider the enormous amount of correctional language throughout the letter.

Correctional Language with 1st Timothy

It talks about lifting up holy hands without wrath or doubting, no doubt linked to hostilities that had risen towards the Christian faith. Specifically, regarding women, the apostle wrote about young widows gossiping and spreading slander. He likewise added that the wife of a bishop was not to be a slanderer. The literal Greek there would translate "no devil", thus stating as a qualification that they're "not an accuser". It makes sense, as by virtue of their status they'd be privy to information that could be used to slander individuals.

Finally, the letter closes with correctional language about people who are driven by a lust for money. When you consider that two of the major villains ("Alexander the coppersmith" and "Demetrius the silversmith") that the apostle Paul encountered while living in Ephesus were of that persuasion, this is a point that is well worth making.

One villainous man who was tied to his love of money that likewise lived in the vast metropolis of Ephesus was named Demetrius. By trade, he was a silver smith. When Demetrius felt that his livelihood of crafting idols was in jeopardy, he rallied the other idol makers together. They then rallied the crowds, which created an angry mob. Seeking to kill Paul but unable to find him, they instead apprehended Gaius and Aristarchus. This explosive account is detailed in the nineteenth chapter of Acts. This event marked the end of Paul's four-year stay in the city of Ephesus. He left there bidding his friends Timothy, Priscilla, Aquila, and others who resided there, goodbye.

The correctional language along with the history both recorded in the Bible and history set a clear tone relating to problematic issues inside Ephesus. Knowing that Ephesus was home of the Temple of Artemus, which was one of the seven wonders of the world, and notably the most lavish of them all, it's easy to understand why someone would immediately question the context of 1st Timothy 2:9-15. After all, Ephesus was a city long built around Goddess culture, and was also directly associated with the Amazons of Greek myth.

The Ephesians history of Goddess worship is vastly more complex than just the worship of Artemis. It was a city that was long colonized. Archeology dates inhabitants of Ephesus all the way back to the Neolithic Era. However, it was during the Bronze Age where they found Goddess worship was prevalent there. In the same location as the temple of Artemis, there had afore lied a temple to the goddess Kebala.

Contrary to the traditional Greek or Roman portrayals of their goddess Artemis (Greek)/Diana (Roman), which are the same, the Ephesian variation, is a clear infusion of one feminine deity with another. Like Kebala, their version of Artemis is a mother goddess figure. It's a specific classification of female deity of which only a few fall into. Worshipping her as the mother goddess role, and especially infusing her character with the goddess Kebala only adds that much more fire to the tone of this Ephesus' goddess culture.

Does The Bible Practice What It Preaches?

Beyond the points of what was going on cul-
turally, a non-Greek speaking Christian who isn't a
theologian but reads and retains their Bible might
question perceivable contradictions. Whereas the
Bible doesn't contradict itself, and as a Christian we
believe what Paul was writing here was inspired by
the Holy Spirit, it's easy to ask questions revolving
around 1st Timothy 2:2. After all, the same apostle
Paul who wrote *"But I suffer not a woman to teach"*
also commended Priscilla, a woman, for teaching
(Acts 18:26). The same apostle Paul regarded Junia,
the wife of Andronicus who were of note among the
apostles (Romans 16:7), which may have very well
meant they were apostles?

The same Bible has God calling Deborah to
be a judge over all of Israel in an olden time, which
was even more discriminatory towards women.
Whereas she was clearly in charge over everyone,
was Deborah usurping authority over men? In Micah
6:4, Miriam is equated as a prophet mentioned side
by side with both Moses and Aaron. Was Miriam who
was exalted by God to this status usurping authority
over men? Was the elect lady of the church that the
second epistle of John was written to usurping authority over a man? Likewise, can you fathom the
importance that woman had within the church to
receive a letter? By virtue of the fact that church

leadership were the recipients of letters of this nature, should it not be indicative that this woman was a pastor or overseer much like Junia, Deborah, Miriam were leaders?

These are honest questions that anyone knowing a thimble's worth of the Bible could easily ask himself or herself. The question is, if women aren't supposed to ever teach then why was Paul praising Priscilla, who lived in Ephesus and had church meetings in her home with her husband Aquila? If it were a damnable thing for a woman to ever be in charge of men period, then why do we find God putting them there over and over again in the Bible?

It's very well known that scripture burns the barriers of gender, race, and nationality to the ground in saying, *"There is neither Jew nor Greek, there is neither bond nor free, there is neither male nor female: for ye are all one in Christ Jesus."* (Galatians 3:28) Considering all of these points, and the many others that we've yet to cover, regarding how the Bible itself endorses women in ministry, how can the apostle Paul come back around and war against it? Is that what he's doing? Is he still a Pharisee at heart? What exactly is going on in these verses?

What is Paul saying specifically in Greek?

Thirdly, the other way of questioning this is by asking, "What was Paul really saying, in the language he was saying it in, without any words being obscured within the English translation?" Quite honestly, all three of these methods of analyzing scripture all lead you to the same answer, that Paul wasn't damning women who God has called into ministry.

The Greek language is extremely specific. In the English language I could say, "I love my wife, I love my church, I love God, I love a coworker, and I love key lime pie". Whereas in English I'm using the same word, it's meaning is changing. In Greek, I'd not be using the same vague word, but different words to emphasize what kind of love I was talking about.

Paul's Letter to the church at Corinth

As previously mentioned in this chapter, scriptures found within the first epistle to Timothy are not the only passages in the Bible utilized to favor the suppression or rejection of women in ministry. In addition to it, Paul's letter to the Corinthians states:

"Let your women keep silence in the churches: for it is not permitted unto them to speak; but they are commanded to be under obedience, as also saith the law. And if they will learn any thing, let them ask their husbands at home: for it is a shame for women to speak in the church." (1st Corinthians 14:34-35)

The Corinthian church was fiery. By today's standards people could easily equate this church to the Pentecostal or charismatic churches. Chapters 12-14 are a commentary directly related to the gifts of the spirit, all of which abounded within the church at Corinth. Chapter 12 enumerates the gifts. Chapter 13 confronts the people saying that though they have the infilling of the Holy Spirit and are blessed with the manifestation of spiritual gifts, which are utilized as an outward sign to the unbeliever, that without love they're meaningless.

Chapter 12 proceeds to speak of the ongoing existence of the gifts of the Spirit until Christ's return (1 Cor. 13:10). In the fourteenth chapter of Corinthians the Bible deals explicitly with the subject of speaking in tongues. The entire chapter is devoted to the subject. Beyond it's uses of application, the apostle Paul is calling for a sense of order, stating, "Let all things be done in decency and order". It's in the midst of instructing this vivacious spiritual church as to how they should conduct themselves that he makes the statement found in 1st Corinthians 14:34-35.

Again, just like before the decreeing reader could ask a myriad of questions & likely should. If the apostle Paul's message to women in 1st Cor. 14:34 was "Shut up", then why was he talking about women wearing head coverings while they prayed and prophesied in church three chapters earlier? In and of itself that fact alone in the same letter to the same church makes it vividly clear that 1st Cor. 14:34 is not a gag order pronounced on the totality of womankind, nor is he prohibit-

ing women from praying or prophesying in the church of
Corinth.

CHAPTER 2:
JESUS GETS ALL THE
GOOD WOMEN

Before I was born there stood a small church on Alexis Road in Sylvania, Ohio that was owned by the Pentecostal Church of Christ. For clarity, this was prior to their organization being renamed the International Pentecostal Church of Christ. As it was a small church with only a few individuals in attendance, it was not a church that many ministers desired to have. Faithfully, Rev. Hazel Fannon pastored the small church for years. She pastored when there were but a few. She pastored when it was just she and her family. Without any sort of financial compensation, nor any real accolade, she was faithful in keeping a church open that otherwise would have closed.

Proceeding Rev. Hazel Fannon's pastorship, the church was then pastored by Rev. Herald Evans, followed by Rev. Jess Hurley, and finally Rev. Ozzie Vincent. Pastor Vincent was the last minister within the Pentecostal Church of Christ to pastor the small church. Around the time that Rev. Vincent had began, my Mother Jonelle Blankenship and Father Larry Blankenship gave their hearts to the Lord in that church. It was a church whose doors perhaps would not have remained open, if it were not for a woman stepping into the place where God had called her.

Throughout the course of time there have been several sorts of people who have been left out of the history books, the losers, the disabled, the poor, and women. History has been written by the victors. History has been written by men. In addition to this, women have been widely discriminated against across many societies and throughout religiosity. In contrast to this, the Bible continuously displays God's egalitarian way of thinking in relation to gender.

After all, women are mentioned in the genealogy of Jesus Christ. The earliest of those was Tamar. In the account of her life she married Judah's son Er, but Er was a wicked man so God killed him. According to the law the next brother in line was supposed to marry his brother's widow and thereby take care of her. She then married Judah's son Onan. I could not over express the importance of the then coming messiah, which in Christianity we recognize as Jesus Christ. This was the biggest deal of all, yet Onan was abusive and neglectful of Tamar. He was unwilling to procreate. Whatever the extent of their sexual relations, the Bible tells us that he'd spill his semen on the ground. His disregard for God's command, "Be fruitful and multiply", his lack of concern towards the coming messiah, and the mistreatment of his wife (Tamar) are a testament of his life. Due to his wickedness God saw Onan, a son of Judah; dead.

As odd as it may seem, she was then waiting for the younger son to be of age to marry her in hopes that she'd be taken care of. After all she was already a part of this family. That day never came. Rejected and disregarded like trash, Tamar had a plan. She dressed like a temple prostitute. Temple prostitution was a practice associated with paganism, which was forbidden to the Jewish people. They did however partake in it during various years of their apostasy.

With her face veiled Judah found her and unknowingly slept with his sons widow Tamar. After having sex with her, Judah went to fetch her a goat as payment. As a show of good faith, she asked him to leave his signet ring and staff. He did so and left. Upon his return, she was gone. When asking people as to the whereabouts of the temple prostitute, they told him that they did not have a temple prostitute in their town.

Months later, Tamar began to show. When the self-righteous Judah heard that she was pregnant, he was enraged. Mistreated, neglected, and abused Tamar's life was now hanging by a thread. When accusations were made as to whom she had sex with outside of marriage, she sent Judah's staff and signet ring back to him with the message saying, "This is the man who I have laid with." Filled with remorse and tears in his eyes,

Judah exclaimed that Tamar was more righteous than he.

Far removed from the love that God had towards women like Tamar, in many men's eyes they were downcast. The Jewish historian and traitor, Josephus made his views clear on women in writing, *"A woman is inferior to her husband in all things"* (Josephus, Against Apion, Book 2, Sec. 25) Philo of Alexandria's view on women were also penned numerable times, one of which states, *"Wives must be slaves to their husbands."* (Philo, Hypothetic 7.3) Despite this misguided anti-Biblical way of thinking, the synoptic gospel turned this way of thinking on its ear.

The next woman named within the genealogy of Jesus Christ was Rahab; a harlot who lived in house built into the walls of Jericho. It was there she aided and abetted an Israelite scouting party. God saved her along with her family, and they converted to Judaism.

Next, we find Ruth. The book bearing her name tells us the story of this woman. During a time of famine, a Jewish family left their home in Bethlehem Judah and transplanted themselves to the pagan land of Moab. It was there that their sons married. As the years went by, things became good in Bethlehem Judah, Naomi's husband and sons had died. She told her sons widows that she was going home. Clearly, an impact had been made on Ruth by this family. She exclaimed to Naomi that Naomi's people were her people, and Naomi's God was her god.

Pulled from paganism Ruth eventually finds herself marrying Boaz. The book of Ruth is a beautiful story of romance and God's redeeming grace. In an age where women's names escaped the face of time, we find them holding their own in the pages of the Bible.

Finally, within Jesus genealogy; Bathsheba is named. She initially was the wife of an honorable man named Uriah. One night while on his balcony King David saw her slipping out into the night to take a purification bath. This was a Jewish ritual signifying that she'd ended her monthly period.

With lust in his heart, David sent for her. He slept with and impregnated Bathsheba, tried to cover it up, had Uriah killed in battle, and thought he'd gotten away with it. Despite all of his wonderful qualities this was a moment of weakness in the life of David. A prophet sent by God came to him, revealed what he had done, and pronounced judgment from the Lord upon him. While there were many bitter harvests from the seeds David had sewn there was love and forgiveness. David and Bathsheba lost their first baby, but eventually had a son who would reign as the next king. His name was Solomon.

In a world where women have been dismissed, overlooked, ridiculed and scorned merely for being fe-male, Jesus Christ personified the character of God by treating womankind of equal value to their male coun-terparts. Within the Judaic religious society women were regarded as second-class citizens. An oral tradition which was taught and eventually penned said, *"It is bet-ter that the words of the Law should be burned than that they should be given to a woman."* (Talmud; Tractate J.

Sotah, 3.4; 19a) For scholarly reference do note that passage was written within the Jerusalem Talmud, and later omitted from the Babylonian Talmud.

In spite of how religious society downgraded women, Jesus Christ went out of his way to reach them with the Gospel. In the fourth chapter of John it's recorded that Jesus intentionally travelled out of his way to bring salvation to a Samaritan woman who was drawing water from a well. When Jesus' mother Mary came with his half-brothers to speak with Him, He took the opportunity gesturing to the crowd that was about him and responding, *"Behold my mother and my brethren! For whosoever shall do the will of God, the same is my brother, and my sister, and mother."* (MARK 3:34b-35). Within that passage he was demonstrating an equal acknowledgement toward the female disciples as well as the males.

Many of Christ's disciples were women. They listened to and followed his teachings. Likewise, they contributed to the ministry just as the male disciples did. The Bible notes this on several occasions, making statements such as, *"And it came to pass afterward, that he went throughout every city and village, preaching and shewing the glad tidings of the kingdom of God: and the twelve were with him, and certain women, which had been healed of evil spirits and infirmities, Mary called Magdalene, out of whom went seven devils, And Joanna the wife of Chuza Herod's steward, and Susanna, and many others, which ministered unto him of their substance."* (Luke 8:1-3)

While the multitudes had abandoned Jesus, it was the Apostle John and a number of female disciples who were at the cross in faithful loving support. Scripture states:

"And many women were there beholding afar off, which followed Jesus from Galilee, ministering unto him: 56A-mong which was Mary Magdalene, and Mary the mother of James and Joses, and the mother of Zebedee's children." (MATTHEW 27:55-56)

"There were also women looking on afar off: among whom was Mary Magdalene, and Mary the mother of James the less and of Joses, and Salome;(Who also, when he was in Galilee, followed him, and ministered unto him;) and many other women which came up with him unto Jerusalem." (MARK 15:40-41)

"And all his acquaintance, and the women that followed him from Galilee, stood afar off, beholding these things." (LUKE 23:49)

"Now there stood by the cross of Jesus his mother, and his mother's sister, Mary the wife of Cleophas, and Mary Magdalene." (JOHN 19:25)

Again, we find that it was the women who accompanied the body of Jesus to the tomb. (MATT 27:61; MARK 15:47; LUKE 23:55) We find that it was women who went to the tomb after the Sabbath at dawn. (MATT 28:1; MARK 16:1; LUKE 24:10; John 20:1) On numerous occasions Christ stood head to head with the Pharisees and Sadducees gross legalism and male chauvinism, of which he was never so much as tempted to join in.

During this same time in history there was a very popular rabbi named Hellel. Essentially, his teachings were that a man could divorce his wife for any cause. According to his teachings trivial things allowed a husband to divorce his wife. If she had bad breath, if she burnt dinner, if he found a woman who he felt was more attractive than his wife are just several examples of the sorts of things that made divorce justifiable. It was a vile doctrine that suited a large number of people and was very well known amongst the Jewish community.

In the nineteenth chapter of Matthew we read of an account where a Pharisee seeking to tear down Jesus in the eyes of the people asked Him the question, "Is it lawful for a man to put away his wife for every cause?" The key to the Pharisee's phrasing of the question is not merely in that it was over the issue of divorce, but more to the point he was asking if a man could divorce his wife for any imaginable reason. As usual, Jesus answered perfectly.

Jesus replied by asking them the question, "What did Moses teach you?" It was a question they verbally dodged, to which Jesus replied by quoting the Torah. They then contested His answer in asking why Moses allowed for a bill of divorcement. Jesus explained that because of the sinfulness of the people's hearts Moses suffered the people to do this. Jesus added, "And I say unto you, whosoever shall put away his wife, except it be for fornication, and shall marry another, committeth adultery: and whoso marrieth her which is put away doth commit adultery." (MARK 10:9)

A hush fell over the crowd. In astonishment Jesus disciples retorted, "His disciples said unto him, If the case of the man be so with his wife, it is not good to marry." In complete contrast to the misogynistic idiocy embraced by some men, Jesus Christ in accordance with scripture expressed that women have value.

Judaic oral tradition teaches, "...He that talks much with women brings evil upon himself, neglects the study of the Torah, and at last will inherit Gehenna." (Talmud; Tractate M. Aboth, 1.5; cf. Nedarim, 20a), yet Jesus turned the Godless doctrines of men on their ear. In regards to women Flavius Josephus wrote, *"This is a governing principle; Any evidence which a woman is not valid [to offer testimony], also they are not valid [to offer testimony]."* (Josephus, War 5.2) Despite viewpoints like this we find the Gospel filled with women. Anna and Simeon prophesied in the temple that the baby Jesus was the Messiah. Running back from the empty tomb, Mary Magdalene was the first to deliver the message of Christ's resurrection.

Speaking of Jesus Christ in relation to women:

"Jesus was a friend of women, the first and practically the last friend women had in the church." (Uta Ranke-Heinemann)

"They [women] had never known a man like this Man - there never has been such another. A prophet and a teacher who never nagged at them, never flattered or coaxed or patronized…who took their questions and arguments seriously; who never mapped out their sphere for them, never urged them to be feminine or jeered at them for being female; who had no axe to grind and no uneasy male dignity to defend; who took them as he found them and was completely unself-conscious." (Dorothy Sayers, Are Women Human? IVP, 47)

"Jesus Christ raised women above the condition of mere slaves, mere ministers to the passions of the man, raised them by His sympathy, to be Ministers of God." (Florence Nightingale)

CHAPTER 3:
YOU'RE EITHER WITH US,
OR EPHESUS!!!

The New Testament's canonical book entitled 1st Timothy is alleged to have been written by the Apostle Paul sometime between 58AD-65AD; between twenty-five to thirty-five years after the death, burial, and resurrection of Jesus Christ. It was a letter directed to Timothy, who oversaw the church in Ephesus on the shores of the Angolan coast with its harbor accessible to the Aegean Sea.

While Pergamon was the capital city of Asia Minor during the Hellenistic period, Ephesus was by American standards its New York City. The city Ephesus had an expansive odeon which seated 1400 guests for an array of musical concerts held there. It had two agoras, which are gathering places where individuals could come gather together at these forums to discuss the civic and commercial affairs. This sizable city had aqueducts, bathhouses, a brothel, gymnasiums, as well as a myriad of attractions and amenities to offer the estimated 250,000-300,000 people who called it their home in the first century AD.

According to tradition, Ephesus was the last home of Jesus mother, Mary. There she was taken care of by the Apostle John. Years after the Apostle Paul's death, the Roman Emperor Domitian; would erect a statue of himself to be worshipped by the inhabitants of the town. This is where The Apostle John refused to take part in the worship and was sentenced to death by boiling in oil. After surviving that, he was exiled to the Isle of Patmos where he penned the book of Revelation.

The crowning achievement amidst the cities Greco-Roman architecture was the Temple of Artemus. This historically renowned temple was not only one of the Seven Wonders of the World, but described as the most glorious. In it's history, it had been destroyed and rebuilt three times. Each time the temple was larger and more elaborate than the time before. The third and final building of the temple was financed by Alexander the Great. Work began on it in 323 BC. The Temple of Artemus was 450' long, 225' wide, and 60' high, and it had perpetual forest of more than 127 columns within it.

Ephesus was a city built around the cult worship of the divine feminine. However, in contrast to how Artemus/Diana is generally portrayed, it's clear that the Ephesian variation of the Greek/Roman triple goddess was infused with Phrygian Mother Goddess, Cybele of Anatolia. In addition to its deity, the city was also specifically linked to the mythos of the Amazons. Those factors as well as others found both Biblically and historically collectively paint a backdrop to the heavily populated seaside locale.

Archaeologists have found signs of inhabitation dating back to the Neolithic period within the city of Ephesus. During the Bronze Age located in the exact place where the temple was erected to the goddess Artemis, there lied the temple to the goddess Cybele. During the second Punic wars (218BC-201BC) she'd be ushered into Greek and Roman culture by the advisement of both the sibylline oracles and the oracle of Delphi. Cybele was known as the "magna mater" (i.e. "great mother"), of which her cult was also named.

She was recognized as the mother of the gods. Her origins are that she was born of a rock, or mountain. Her character is forceful, and associated with the wilds of untainted nature. Often, she is portrayed either sitting between two lions, or in a chariot which is drawn by two lions. In mythology, she is heavily associated with Attis.

Her priests would have to castrate and effeminize themselves. There would be bloodlettings from men on her altar. Later in Roman times castration and such were outlawed, which lead them to the sacrifices of bulls and goats. Cybele's priest would stand beneath the floor where a bull was being slaughtered. After it's death he'd arise to the stage drenched in its blood.

Within Rome, there were two festivals were held which revolved around Cybele. Holy Week (March 15-28) and Megalesia (April 4-10). Whereas the ancient Roman festival of holy week certainly has some involvement regarding Cybele, the primary purpose of this festival is in regard to the birth, death, and resurrection her hermaphroditic pagan priestly deity, Attis. On the first day of the festival, they pay tribute to how the child Attis was found in the reeds along the Sangrias River in Phrygia. On the second day an arbor tree is cut down and paraded along with an image of Attis bound to it, thus symbolizing his death beneath a pine tree. On the third day, the tree is laid to rest at the temple of magna mater. On the fourth day people violently beat and cut themselves mourning the death of Attis. The following day is a day of rejoicing at the resurrection of Attis, followed by a day of rest, a ceremonial day of washing and worship. Finally, the Roman Holy Week ends with men being initiated into the priest hood of the cult of Magna Mater, when legal by blood and castration.

It has been alleged that Attis may have been the title given to Cybele's priests in Phrygia. According to myth, it was he that created her Galli priesthood. The highlight of each year within Magna Mater was the festival of Megalesia. There the Galli priests would dance wildly with knifes in their long yellow robes to the beating of drums and shrill flutes.

Cybele was celebrated as the great mother and mother of the gods. She was worshipped as the divine feminine, and infused with the goddess Artemis of Ephesus.

The goddess Artemis was the byproduct of one of Zeus' many extramarital affairs. She was the daughter of Leto, and the sister of Apollo. She was generally portrayed as a young lady ranging from 12-19 years of age. She carried a bow and arrows, and often wore a crown shaped like the crescent moon. She was the goddess of the moon, night, witchcraft, etc. Artemis guarded young girls, and delivered babies safely. She's associated with a variety of trees, and loved to hunt. An animal that was sacred to her were deer. Her hunting dogs were given to her by the lesser deity Pan.

Artemis vowed to always be a virgin. Despite this she fell in love with a hunter named Orion. To aid his sister in keeping her chastity, Apollo tricked her into shooting Orion with one of her arrows. The goddess grievously mourned, and in tribute to his memory she placed a constellation of Orion and his faithful dog in the heavens.

There are many legends surrounding the mythos of Artemis. Another of such is that a young hunter named Actœon came upon her while she was bathing. What he said varies from story to story. In one he declared her beauty, in another telling of this tale he boasted that he was a greater hunter than she. Regardless, it ended with him being magically transformed into a stag for his indiscretion and ripped to bits by dogs.

Her lore is expansive. She sent a wild boar to kill Adonis. She tricked the wicked twin sons of Poseidon and Iphidemia, named Otos and Ephialtes into killing each other, as it was the only way they could die. Artemus and her brother Apolo executed Queen Niobe's children, of whom the queen felt were more worthy to be worshipped than the gods.

There were several festivals that had direct involvement with the goddess Artemis. According to myth she had tamed a bear that lived near the town of Brauron. People would feed the bear, be kind to the bear, and perhaps even pet the bear. One day several boys killed it, which invoked the wrath of Artemis and therewith caused a plague. To appease her anger a yearly festival was held where young girls would dress in saffron robes and like bears.

Her Ephesian temple was splendorous, and quite notably she was the goddess that they praised. Due to it, people would travel from far and wide to visit, burn incense, and worship. Merchants, local businesses, and idol makers would seek to prosper. One such man was named in the Bible: Demetrius the silver smith. Demetrius lived in Ephesus, was an idol maker, and feared that the Apostle Paul would damage his enterprise with the message of he preached.

In the time of the Roman Empire the heavily populated city of Ephesus had a large medical school. The school was fixed around the snake cult, and Asklepios, the son of Apollo and god of medicine. Outside of their gymnasium there was a statue of the god Hermes, who invented the sports of boxing and racing. Additionally, according to the mythos; Ephesus was home to Ephos, queen of the Amazons.

Far removed from 21st century thinking, it was another time, another place, and another world than we live in today. These were but a few of the cultural aspects revolving around that great city. It was there that Pricilla and Aquila taught the gospel more clearly to the fervent preacher Apollos. It was in Ephesus that the seven sons of Sceva attempted to cast an evil spirit out of a demoniac. The seven are described as vagabonds and exorcists. According to scripture, their father Sceva was a Jew and chief of the priests.

The men rebuked the spirit declaring, "We adjure you by Jesus whom Paul preacheth." As the term vagabond infers, they were not what they should be. The devil spoke out of the man saying, "Jesus I know, and Paul I know; but who are ye?" In that moment, it leaped out of the man that was possessed, and began beating all seven of the vagabonds viciously. The level of the brutality and horror in what unfolded can only be left to the expanse of our imaginations. The Bible indicates the severity of it in recording that they all left that place naked and wounded.

It was then that the fear of God came upon the pagans of the city. A mass book burning was held for all of their books on sorcery and the occult. They counted the price of the books burnt to be worth 50,000 pieces of silver.

While it's a story that's often glazed over with historical and scholarly points evaded, there are several issues surrounding the episode with the seven sons of Sceva. One point that could be brought into question is, "Who exactly was Sceva and what was he a chief priest of?" The likely answer is that terminology used regarding him as a chief priest isn't exclusive to priest within Judaism. The high priests were well documented, so we know he wasn't that. To help with this time line: Saul of Tarsus was born in 5AD, Saint Stephen was martyred in around 35AD, and the Apostle Paul was martyred sometime between 64AD-67AD. As it's clearly indicated, Sceva was not a high priest in regard to Judaism, which leads us to believe that he was a defected Jew (i.e. as Jew by ethnicity only) and a pagan priest. This timeline is reflective of all the high priests who held office during the lifetime of the Apostle Paul.

HIGH PRIEST:	YEARS OF SERVICE:
• Joshua ben Sie	3 BC - ?
• Joazar ben Boethus	? - 6 AD
• Ananus ben Seth	6AD-15AD
• Ishmael ben Fabus (Phiabi)	15AD-16AD
• Eleazar ben Ananus	16AD-17AD
• Simon ben Camithus	17AD-18AD
• Joseph ben Caiaphas	18AD-36AD
• Jonathan ben Ananus	36AD-37AD
• Theophilus ben Ananus	37AD-41AD
• Simon Cantatheras ben Boethus	41AD-43AD
• Matthias ben Ananus	43AD
• Elioneus ben Simon Cantatheras	43AD-44AD

- Jonathan ben Ananus (restored)   44AD
- Josephus ben Camydus   44AD-46AD
- Ananias son of Nedebeus   46AD-58AD
- Jonathan   58AD
- Ishmael II ben Fabus   58AD-62AD
- Joseph Cabi ben Simon   62AD-63AD
- Ananus ben Ananus   63AD
- Jesus son of Damneus   63AD
- Joshua ben Gamla   63AD-64AD
- Mattathias ben Theophilus   65AD-66AD
- Phannias ben Samuel   67AD-70AD

      Another reasonable conclusion about regarding the specific account with the seven sons of Sceva, who were regarded as vagabond Jews and exorcists is that perhaps they imagined that the Apostle Paul was just performing some sort of magic ritual. For those who've studied the occult, you know that knowing a demon's name is supposed to be a significant thing. Considering this line of thought perhaps they reasoned that they could invoke the name of Jesus Christ as a means to expel the evil spirit that possessed the man.

      As the demon had leapt out of the man, and overtaken the seven sons of Sceva causing them to leave naked and wounded, this only further validated the gospel of
Jesus Christ. The call was not, nor is not to include Jesus into your life, but to repent.

After the mass book burning, Demetrius the silver-smith became panicked. He rallied the other idol makers and told them that the growth of this new doctrine could shut them down and even shut down the Temple of Artemus. As it is though roughly recorded in scripture they unified, and formed a riotous mob.

Understanding the background of Ephesus holds significant bearing in regard to shedding light on the letters: "1st Timothy", "2nd Timothy", "Ephesians", and likewise the personal letter dictated by Jesus Christ to their church which was penned by the Apostle John in "Revelation 2:1-6". When the Biblical writers wrote, they left subtle nuances that the readers of that day would understand. Such as 1st Timothy 4:8 says, "For bodily exercise profiteth little: but godliness is profitable unto all things, having promise of the life that now is, and of that which is to come." Within their culture exercise meant far more than that. Boxing and racing were created by the god Hermes/Mercury whose statue stood outside of their gymnasium in Ephesus.

1st Timothy is bombarded with correctional language. Throughout the letter it mentions young widows slandering and gossiping. Considering this a reasonable argument could be made in questioning that in Paul writing: *"In like manner also, that women adorn themselves in modest apparel, with shamefacedness and sobriety; not with braided hair, or gold, or pearls, or costly array; But (which becometh women professing godliness) with good works. Let the woman learn in silence with all subjection. But I suffer not a woman to teach, nor to usurp authority over the man, but to be in silence. For Adam was first formed, then Eve. And Adam was not deceived, but the woman being deceived was in the transgression. Notwithstanding she shall be saved in childbearing, if they continue in faith and charity and holiness with sobriety."* (1st Timothy 2:9-15)

This was not some blindly written letter, nor did the Apostle Paul go into some sort of trance while writing. It was spirit lead, yet with conscious thought towards the surrounding situation. That is the same reason why the synoptic gospels all have a different tone. They weren't written by the same person, but different individuals under the leading of the Holy Spirit, hence their varying points of emphasis and personalities.

As a side note, the Ephesian variation of Artemus is also thought to have roots relating to Astaroth, Astarte, Ishtar, etc.

CHAPTER 4:
THE APOSTLE PAUL AND
THE GIRLS

Considering the Apostle Paul's speech within 1st Timothy 2:9-15 & 1st Corinthians 14:34-35 in regard to women, we could reasonably ask several questions. While seemingly in the 21st century that's a faint concept, the terminology for this is hermeneutics. Often, in this modern age I've come to the distinct opinion that many people in the pews and even more sadly, in the pulpits; swallow up perpetually anything they hear a minister say without any level of evaluation or study.

Let's face it; we're living in a society that is training people not to think. There are so many distractions to draw our focus from any of the things that really do matter in this world. There's also some level of selfishness toward any issue that does not directly involve us. Frankly, in writing this book I have no foreseeable thing to gain. I'm a man, who is likely making any misogynist, unlearned, or misinformed people angry by even writing this book.

It's wildly inappropriate for anyone to isolate specific scriptures, take them out of context, and say we're preaching the perfect word of God. People who've done that have walked into all sorts of craziness. Isolating, magnifying, and taking scripture out of context is exactly why snake-handling churches handle snakes. They read, "And these signs shall follow them that believe; In my name shall they cast out devils; they shall speak with new tongues; They shall take up serpents; and if they drink any deadly thing, it shall not hurt them; they shall lay hands on the sick, and they shall recover." (MARK 16:17-18) - and conclude they're supposed to handle snakes.

Certainly, we see a multitude of these things mentioned within these verses in practice in the New Testament and throughout church history. Where do we see this application specifically in regard to the taking up of serpents? There is no Biblical evidence that people went out and gathered poisonous snakes, put them in a box, and once the music started playing, and they were nice and mesmerized, took them out and danced around the church with them in hand. In fact, the only Biblical example where we see this in practice is after the Apostle Paul is shipwrecked on an island, adding wood to a fire, when suddenly a viper comes out of nowhere and bites him. He both killed the snake in response to the bite and was unscathed by the supernatural power of God.

Again, regarding snake handling we could ask ourselves, "Are we are not called to prove ourselves by our works?" The answer in regard to scripture is a clear, "No". We read in the Bible when Satan approached Jesus asking him to prove who he was by some death-defying feat Jesus refused. In that account, Satan knowingly took scripture out of context to justify false doctrine to Jesus. He isolated Psalm 91:12. Jesus understanding scripture rebutted siting, *"Ye shall not tempt the LORD your God, as ye tempted him in Massah."* (Deuteronomy 6:16) What I don't feel that everyone gets is that if Jesus Christ would have done something to validate who he was before Satan, then we'd have to as well. While certainly our outward deeds and actions are indicative of who and what we are, they're not the root of it, but the fruit (a byproduct) of our spiritual status.

What is strange is how people can be so observant in regard to looking at the Bible in an analytical manner like this regarding the taking up of serpents, but yet they don't apply those same methods to 1st Timothy 2:9-15 & 1st Corinthians 14:34-35. The certainty is that when you put scripture to scripture, those verses are not saying "No Women Preachers".

Before tackling what Paul said in his letter to Timothy, lets first tackle what he was saying to the church at Corinth, as it's shorter and easier. Paul wrote, *"Let your women keep silence in the churches: for it is not permitted unto them to speak; but they are commanded to be under obedience, as also saith the law. 35And if they will learn any thing, let them ask their husbands at home: for it is a shame for women to speak in the church."* (1st Corinthians 14:34-35)

In addressing his statement "Let your women keep silence in the churches", it'd be ignorant to think that the Apostle was saying that women could not audibly speak in church, as we know that three chapters earlier Paul was conveying beliefs in regard to women wearing a head covering in church while they prayed and prophesied in church. Understanding that, we'd be taking scripture out of context if we took this to mean that women were to be completely hushed.

Simply put, the entire context revolves around how the men and women did not sit together in their church services. The men were educated while the women of that day were housewives. It was a call for order, so that women weren't disrupting the service belting out questions to their husbands across the sanctuary while the speaker was teaching. This is why the passage indicates "*...if they (women) will learn any thing, let them ask their husbands at home."*

Separate seating between men and women was not, nor is not an uncommon practice within some cultures and time periods. Men and women have notably sat apart from one another in Islamic, Sikh, Orthodox Jewish, Coptic Christian, Amish, many Hindu and Jain worship services. At the Wailing Wall in Jerusalem men and women pray in different areas. Paul's plea for order within the Corinthian church no doubt stems from situations that may have been arising.

The reasons that churches put up on their monitors, "please silence your cellphones" isn't out of a want, but necessity. It's something that shouldn't have to be said. You could easily exclaim that there is no way that people could be that ignorant, irreverent, and/or disrespectful to have their cellphones going off in church. However, being a pastor, from my vantage point I can tell you that you're emphatically wrong. It could only be left up to the imagination what certain individuals have scored on Temple Run or Angry Birds while their pastor is delivering their hard studied 45-minute (give or take) Sunday morning sermon.

In a postmodern era where information abounds, common sense is not that common any more. That is why churches, movie theaters, etc. advise people not to interrupt a presentation by causing a distraction by messing with their cellphone. Sadly, it has to be said. In addition, I'd be lying if I denied that in the back of my mind I've imagined putting certain laity up to speak, sitting on the front row and ravaging a bag of Sun Chips just to let them know how it sometimes feels to be a pastor and disrespected so.

Paul's letter to Timothy goes into a few more things, and thus greater depth. He writes: *"In like manner also, that women adorn themselves in modest apparel, with shamefacedness and sobriety; not with braided hair, or gold, or pearls, or costly array; But (which becometh women professing godliness) with good works. Let the woman learn in silence with all subjection. But I suffer not a woman to teach, nor to usurp authority over the man, but to be in silence. For Adam was first formed, then Eve. And Adam was not deceived, but the woman being deceived was in the transgression. Not-*

withstanding she shall be saved in childbearing, if they continue in faith and charity and holiness with sobriety." (1st Timothy 2:9-15)

If you don't think people trip all over this, then it's likely that you don't think. There are cultures in the world where Christian ministers have misunderstood this text and told women that having lots and lots of children is a fundamental part of their salvation. I heard a story dictated by a certain very well-known preacher who was on the mission field preaching a sermon on these verses. When he expounded on the meaning of the 15th verse a hush fell over the crowd. The interpreter stopped interpreting. There was a tension in the air. A minister pulled him aside, and explained to him what they'd always believed this verse meant. Furthermore, he exhibited an abundance of stress because he'd have to tell all of these precious women who'd birthed many children while believing that misinterpreted doctrine that they were taught wrong.

Within the Greek text, the words that the Apostle uses are important. When he writes, "Let the woman learn in silence" (1st Timothy 2:11) the word used for silence is ἡσυχία (hēsychia). This specific word does not mean speechless but rather an inner quiet, or a peace within. When we consider the abundance of correctional language in 1st Timothy alone it should be highly understandable why Paul admonished them to essentially "calm down". Further when he's instructing the women especially within that goddess culture society to do so with "submission" (1st Timothy 2:11), he's again insisting that they need to keep themselves under control.

Following this statement, we find the stand alone verse that male chauvinists utilize to say the Bible is in opposition to women preachers, which reads, *"But I suffer not a woman to teach, nor to usurp authority over the man, but to be in silence"* (1st Timothy 2:12) Let's stop to ask some questions as a means of shedding light on this specific verse.

If the Apostle Paul was saying that a woman shouldn't teach, then why did he commend Priscilla for teaching? If a person believed that by "usurp authority over a man" meant that a woman should never be an authority figure in the church, or over men then why did God himself appoint Deborah to be a both a prophetess and judge over all of the Israelites?

"Now Deborah, a prophet, the wife of Lappidoth, was leading[a] Israel at that time. She held court under the Palm of Deborah between Ramah and Bethel in the hill country of Ephraim, and the Israelites went up to her to have their disputes decided. (Judges 4:4-5)

If a person believed that by "usurp authority over a man" meant that a woman should never be an authority figure in the church, or over men then why did God choose to make Miriam a prophetess over Israel who was declared in the same breath with the same tone of respect as both Moses an Aaron, as she is regarded as such by the prophet Micah? *"For I brought thee up out of the land of Egypt, and redeemed thee out of the house of servants; and I sent before thee Moses, Aaron, and Miriam."* (Micah 6:4)

If a woman's word and testimony lack validity then why did God choose to use the prophetess Anna as one of the two witnesses in whom through divine proclamation attested that the Christ child was in fact the messiah?

If a woman is not to "usurp authority over a man" means they're to have no real level of status within the church, then what does scripture mean when it names a woman Junia as being of note among the Apostles? (Romans 16:7)

If a woman is not to have any sort of status or position within the church body then why was the second epistle of John written to a woman, who was regarded as the elder elect lady and her children, as we read in its introductory passage? (2nd John 1:1-3) Certainly, there are these examples and many others of women holding status, publicly teaching, preaching, and prophesying within the church.

While those points all clearly suggest that Paul was not forbidding women from public ministry, a more in-depth explanation to "Usurp" could be drawn from the preceding verse. Usurp has often been found by many Biblical scholars as a pejorative term. The word usurp within the Greek is αὐθεντεῖν (authentein). This word is found only once within the Bible itself, hence Paul was using a very specific word with a very specific meaning. There is a combative military element to it, such as to overtake or to seize. The following verse spreads light on the terminology used as it relates the argument back to Eve.

In the third chapter of Genesis we read of the consequences of sin. Specifically, to the woman, God said, "I will greatly multiply thy sorrow and thy conception; in sorrow thou shalt bring forth children; and thy desire shall be to thy husband, and he shall rule over thee." The Hebrew word for "rule" is יִמְשָׁל (yim-šāl-). This is not a favorable statement, but a curse bringing about contention, and thereby creating a disharmonious friction between the sexes.

If you consider this while looking at Deborah and various other females who God had put in charge, scripture is clear that this is not the Apostle Paul being a legalistic woman hating Pharisee. In fact Paul worked with, ministered with, and praised his sisters in Christ without partiality all the time. I'd personally add that you can't "usurp" something that is given to you.

In spite of all this, some bigoted self-serving men will still hold to the position, "No Women Preachers Ever!" If they're somewhat familiar with 1st Timothy 2 they'll often site it, commonly relating verse 14 as the justification of this, stating, "And Adam was not deceived, but the woman being deceived was in the transgression." It's an interesting point to make, and it is something Paul did say, though within scripture he made a few points regarding the fall of mankind in Eden.

In the book of Genesis, it's recorded that God instructed man that he could eat of any tree in the garden with the exclusion of the tree of the knowledge of good and evil. Later Eve was tricked and coerced by Satan. To the contrary Adam sinned willingly with his eyes wide open. Just like every one of us today, he knew that it was wrong but he did it anyway because he wanted to do it. It's a point that Paul makes in 1st Corinthians 15, relating the fall to the first Adam and referencing Jesus Christ as the second Adam.

Again, and again, scripture doesn't devalue people, but rather even in our lowest states God lovingly lifts us up. Just as Jesus Christ journeyed to the Samaritan woman who had been thrown away by every man she'd been with. Seemingly, her life long journey to find a man who truly knew her as she was and loved her anyway, and when she encountered the Lord Jesus Christ, she did.

God's love is an account that we read of time and time again. Hagar and her young son Ismael were exiled from the camp. As they left tears filled her eyes knowing that they'd die, but God spoke to her. He spoke blessings over her and her son's future, and their ancestors due to their relation to Abraham. While they were cast aside a perfect all-seeing God loved, protected them, and blessed their futures.

In reality, if the Apostle Paul were dismissing women in 1st Timothy 2 & 1st Corinthians 14, it'd only show him to have some sort of severe mental disorder considering the wealth of statements which make it evident that he was favorable to women in ministry. To the church of Galatia, which is also in Angola like Ephesus, Paul wrote, *"There is neither Jew nor Greek, there is neither bond nor free, there is neither male nor female: for ye are all one in Christ Jesus."* (Galatians 3:28)

CHAPTER 5:
MATRIARCHS OF
MINISTRY

Invariably, God's consistent pattern is not to judge externally but to judge righteously looking directly into a person's heart. Just as the Spirit spoke to Samuel not to choose a king for Israel based on Jesse's son's outward appearance, God does not call people based on super-ficial reasons. As many preachers have proclaimed, "God does not call the equipped, God equips the called!"

Scripture tells us to be not conformed to this world but to be transformed by the renewing of our mind. (Romans 12:2) Ideologically, the way we think will govern our actions. While the Greek and Hebrew texts can be picked apart at a granular level over the accents on words and such, the writers and readers from the time that the Pauline Epistles and likewise were written had a firm grasp on what they meant. Noting that point, if the qualification of a deacon means to be the husband of one wife in a literal sense without gender neutrality, then why do we find a deaconess (Phoebe) in Romans 16:1?

Someone clinging to the complementarian view regarding women would dismiss Phoebe, stating that she must have been a deacon's wife. Yet nothing in the Bible would as much as infer such. Within the New Testament the word used for a Deacon or Deaconess (such as Phoebe) is the same Greek word; διάκονος (diakonos). In later times there was a distinctly feminine Greek word used for διακόνισσα (diakonissa). According to the Hexham Bible Dictionary, this feminine variation of the Greek word was initially instituted at the first council of Nicea.

There has been a long history of deaconesses throughout the history of the church. Regarding the history of deaconesses within the church, Dr. Perry Stone writes, *"When the Christian church split between the West (Catholic) and the East (Byzantine, later termed the Orthodox), the Eastern Church permitted women to serve in the position of deaconess. A deaconess was a female who served to help in the work of the ministry. The ministry of a deaconess was mentioned by early fathers Clement of Alexandria and Origen. The deaconess was generally a widow who had only once been married, although sometimes the position was filled by virgins. Christian historians note that the deaconess ministry functions included certain pastoral duties, including* baptizing the female converts in the congregation, caring for those who were imprisoned, and assisting in comforting the persecuted. The deaconess also assisted the women who had given birth to children and visited with members of their own gender.

In the third century, in Syria, a document called *Didascalia of the Apostles* expressed that the bishop *""appoint a woman for the ministry of women. For there are homes in which you cannot send a male deacon to their women, on the account of the heathen, but you may send a deaconess...and there are many other matters the office of a woman deacon is required...""* In the fifth century, the *Apostolic Constitutions recorded a bishop laying hands-on women and calling down the Holy Spirit for the ministry of the diaconate."* (The Perry Stone Hebraic Prophetic Study Bible, 1 Corinthians In Depth, Page 322, by Dr. Perry Stone)

There were numerable women within the Bible who had on going prophetic ministries. We read that Miram, Deborah, Huldah, Anna, Phillips 4 daughters, and the prophet Isaiah's wife were all prophets. (Micah 6:4; Judges 4:4-5; 2nd Kings 22:14; Luke 2:36-37; Act 21:9; Isaiah 8:3) In the New Testament we find a woman named Dorcas or Tabitha (depending on which language), Priscilla teaching, Junia being of note amount the apostles, and elect lady of the church and her children being the recipient of the 2nd epistle of John.

In his letter to Phillipi, Paul writes, *"I beseech Euodias, and beseech Syntyche, that they be of the same mind in the Lord. I intreat thee also, true yokefellow, help those women which labored with me in the gospel, with*

Clement also, and with other my fellow laborers, whose names are in the book of life." (Philippians 4:2-3) Essentially, what we're reading here is that not only did Paul have no qualms with working alongside women for the kingdom of the Lord, but additionally he regarded them equally.

In the fourth chapter of Exodus a rather peculiar sub-story is found within the verses twenty-four through twenty-six. While some Bible students have regarded it as an exegetical nightmare, there is a point of clarity that merits going there. The verses read: *"And it came to pass by the way in the inn, that the LORD met him, and sought to kill him. Then Zipporah took a sharp stone, and cut off the foreskin of her son, and cast it at his feet, and said, Surely a bloody husband art thou to me. So he let him go: then she said, A bloody husband thou art, because of the circumcision.* (Exodus 4:24-26)

While there is an expansive amount of depth, speculation, and research that can be applied to go swirling all around the questions within this story, there are several points that are clear.

1) God was going to kill, either Moses or Moses son Gershom

2) Moses wife, circumcised their son, touched (וַתַּגַּע - wat-tag-ga') the severed foreskin to Moses (לְרַגְלָיו - lə-raḡ-lāw); and somehow that made everything good

3) We know that what Moses wife, Zipporah did was a priestly act, and God accepted it.

Dr. Michael Heiser has alleged a theory that Moses may have been circumcised in an Egyptian fashion, rather than the proper Hebraic way. According to archeology Egyptians circumcised males by slipping the foreskin, rather than completely removing it. Due to Zipporah's heritage (i.e. she was from the lineage of Esau). She knew who God (YHVH) was, and was familiar with the covenant practice of circumcision, etc. Dr. Heiser admittedly theorizes that perhaps in Zipporah touching the foreskin to Moses genitals, she was circumcising him by proxy. Do note that the Hebrew word used for "feet" can also mean the leg or genital region. That same word is also used in the book Ezekiel reading, *"You built yourself a high place at the top of every street and made your beauty abominable, and you spread your legs to every passer-by to multiply your harlotry."* (Ezekiel 16:25, NASV) The KJV interprets that word as feet, though someone's feet are not what are being alluded to in that text.

Regarding Exodus 4:24-26, there has been a great deal of scholarly study and thought. Outside of the three points, which are named above, the rest isn't entirely clear. On this subject of these three verses John I. Durham writes, *"These verses are among the most difficult in the Book of Exodus, not in terms of their translation, which is quite straightforward, but in terms of their meaning and their location in this particular context"* (Exodus, Word Biblical Commentary [Waco, TX: Word, 1987], 56-59).

It should suffice to say that when studying the Hebrew text that it was not Boaz's feet that Ruth uncovered as she lied next to him. Simply put, it was a marriage proposal. She was very clear. Due to her current situation of being betrothed to another man when she loved Boaz, she was forced to make a desperate move. Within this case as well as with Tamar's we find that the cause did justify the means, as they both are found in the genealogy of Jesus Christ.

Within some circles the five women listed in Jesus' genealogy are representational of the five different types of women found in society, whom Christ's love reaches and he calls to himself. Inside this vein of though, Tamar represents the female who was bitter at her circumstances. Ruth is representational of the woman whose circumstances were against her. Rehab represents the women from a completely non-Christian background. Bathsheba represents the woman who loves God but gets drawn into compromising situations. Mary the mother of Jesus represents the woman who has been committed to Christ from her youth.

The sad truth is that the lens that we view the world through often causes us to trivialize or inflate certain elements within stories and life in general. Women have done significant things all throughout the course of history, yet they've often been hydroplaned over as if they were merely marginal events along the highway of human history. What Zipporah did in Exodus 4 within the span of those three verses is likely monumental. If we allege that due to some circumstance that God was going to kill Moses, whom He'd already called to deliver the people from the land of Egypt (for whatever reason) and Zipporah kept God's initial plan regarding His calling over Moses life from going off the rails, that would make this a monumental occurrence. Is it just happenstance that this hermeneutical pothole is placed within Exodus 4? All we really know for certain is that Zipporah did save someone, either Moses or his or her son by performing a priestly rite that God accepted.

We see across the plain of time where women have stepped up when men would not. In the life of David, he met a beautiful intelligent woman named Abigail who was married to an idiot. His name was Nabal, which means fool. (1st Samuel 25) After being a colossal jerk, Nabal suffers a massive stroke or something to that effect, and after three days of paralysis he dies. Two chapters later, David has taken Abigail to be one of his wives.

As the book of 1st Samuel begins we read of a man named Elkanah who had two wives. Of his wives, Hannah was the favorite, yet she was barren. The other woman, whose name was Peninnah, saw Hannah as the enemy within. It's a situation we see played out in the Bible time and time again through the polygamous marriages of the Old Testament. Peninnah was cranking out babies for her husband and rubbing it in Hannah's face that of the two of them she was the wife who was giving her husband heirs and leaving him fulfilled.

Agonizing within, Hannah eventually finds herself at the temple praying, but the words just won't audibly come out. Her story is one of a woman who wants to have a baby. She makes a vow to the Lord that if He'd allow her to have a son that she'd turn the child over to Him. God touches her womb and allows her to become pregnant. It's a miracle birth, and a fundamental part of the story of her son, the prophet Samuel's life.

There are women who have turned the tides of war. Rabbinic writings, which are the presumptions of men downplay things of this nature with statements like, *"Said R. Mordecai to him: ""So said Abimi of Hagrunia, that a man whom a woman has killed must not be taken into consideration.""* (Babylonian Talmud, Chapter 8, pg. 255-256) However, the Bible tells a different tale. In the book of Judges a woman named Jael is mentioned in regards to a war. There, a high-ranking enemy soldier coming by finds what he thinks is refuge and comfort at her lodging. She comes off as kind and sweet. She speaks subtle words of comfort, gives him some warm milk, makes him feel at ease to lie down and rest. While he's asleep, Jael takes a tent spike and drives it through his brain with the metal spike protruding out of his temples and faceting his corpse to the ground. (Judges 4:17-22)

If scripture did not continually illustrate God's acceptance of women within ministry by application, and their equal value then why have questions countering the religious societies complementarianism? In Jewish texts, we read of an account like this saying, *"Come and hear. The proselyte Beluria (a woman) asked R. Gamaliel (concerning the following apparent contradiction): It is written in your Law [Deut. 17]: "The Lord who regardeth not persons" (literally, who lifteth not up countenances); and it is also written [Numb. vi. 26]: "May the Lord lift up his countenance.""* (Babylonian Talmud, New Year, Chapter 1, pg. 30) What immediately happens next is

Rabbi Jose hears the question and swiftly comes in to inject his opinion by way of a parable. Then he tells another parable, which only seems to muddy the waters. R. Jose then injects that initial response within the first parable is that these two verses are talking about two different things. He adds that his opinion is that one of the verses deals with God while the other verse deals with man.

While R. Jose the Galilean's parable and explanation was tactful enough sidestep to put more than a few people off regarding him, perhaps his stance that a writing of divorcement to a woman which is written on a living animal is not lawful should grant him a little grace. This is mentioned in the Talmud specifically because there were other people who felt this was completely legitimate. He and other characters which are Rabbis, Sadducees, Pharisees, etc. converse telling stories, asking questions, imposing laws, and quoting scripture all throughout this ancient Hebrew text. In one place, the Talmud explains that a deaf-mute, an idiot, or a child are forbidden to light the Hanukkah menorah. Understanding all of the man-made standards imposed within the Babylonian Talmud only makes it clearer what kind of spiritualized bigoted religiosity that Jesus Christ was faced with when dealing with the Pharisees and Sadducees.

The Babylonian Talmud is long and in many of its teaching and saying, at its worst points it can range from mentally disturbed, morally lacking, legalistic, or heretical. Regarding the golden rule, "Do unto others as you'd have them do unto you", this passage is warped into a twisted justification of a man seeing his betrothed in the nude to check out the merchandise thus verifying that he's not going to be displeased with her. That passage specifically reads: *"The commandment in the Old Testament (Leviticus xix., 17): "'Love thy neighbor as thyself, '"* the Talmud interprets in a negative sense by the words of Hillel, the elder, thus: ""That which

thou likest not being done unto thyself do not unto thy neighbor,"" and this rule the Talmud

adopts in all the ways of charity, and in all affairs in which man comes in contact with his fellow-man; e.g., based upon this biblical commandment it is forbidden to betroth a woman

before seeing her, for he may dislike her thereafter, and as one does not wish to be disliked

himself, he must not cause another to be

disliked." (Babylonian Talmud, Part II, Ethics of the Talmud, Chapter 1, pg. 82-83)

The Jerusalem Talmud is dramatically more down to earth, and is much shorter in length. The Jerusalem Talmud talks extensively about obligations, and who is obligated to do certain things and who is not. This Judaic liturgy, which was taught by Rabbi Judah, was meant to be prayed by the Jewish man thanking God for not making him a gentile, a boor, or a woman. It states:

[XIII.A] It was taught: R. Judah says, "A person must recite three

blessings each day: 'Blessed [art Thou, O Lord, our God, King of the

Universe,] who did not make me a gentile'; 'Blessed [art Thou, O Lord, our God, King of the Universe,] who did not make me a boor'; 'Blessed

[art Thou, O Lord, our God, King of the Universe,] who did not make me

a woman.'

[B] "[What is the basis for these blessings?] 'Blessed [art Thou, O Lord,

our God, King of the Universe,] who did not make me a gentile,' because

the gentiles are of no matter. [As it says,] 'All the nations are as nothing

before him' [Isa. 40:17].

[C] "'Blessed [art Thou, O Lord, our God, King of the Universe,] who

did not make a boor,' for, A boor does not fear sin [M. Abot 2:5].

[D] "'Blessed [art Thou, O Lord, our God, King of the Universe,] who

did not make me a woman,' for, women are not obligated to perform the

commandments [T. 6:18]."

(Jerusalem Talmud/Yerushalmi Berakhot, Chapter 9, pg. 329)

These were the mindsets of people (i.e. Pharisees and Sadducees) who combatted Jesus Christ. They were the men who brought a woman casting her, likely half naked or fully nude at the feet of Jesus Christ exclaiming how the law of Moses demands she be stoned to death for her sin, then they asked Him the railing question, "But what do you say we should do?"

It's a story that illustrates there is a clearly defined line between that which is self-righteous and that which is righteous. Scripture tells us that Jesus Christ kneeled down and began writing something in the dust. Then he looked up and answered perfectly, "Let him who has no sin cast the first stone." He saved her life, forgave her of her sins, and highlighted the fundamentally important message that sin will either lead us to the feet of Jesus Christ or to Hell. In a society where religion disregarded women, Jesus called them to follow him.

CHAPTER 6:
YES, SHE CAN!

In the postmodern 21st century over half a millennium since the women's liberation movements of the 1960's, women within ministry have become dramatically more common core within many denominational structures. A battle for recognition towards the callings that God has placed on the lives of such women has been long fought and still faces heavy opposition by some. Sadly, though we see again and again clarity in scripture by the application of women throughout ministry, many in the religious world still feel that a fundamental component that makes someone applicable to be in ministry is a penis.

Having been inside the church world all of my life I've seen some horrible, negligent, and incompetent things from pastors. There are men elected or placed in positions of power who do harm to hurting people. Just in talking to people, it's staggering how many say they don't go to church anymore because they've been church hurt. While I believe that everything should be looked at on a case-by-case basis, it'd be illogical to think that every one of these people is wrong.

Our next-door neighbor was the kindest sweetest man. We'd converse every time we'd see each other in passing. Beyond idle conversation, he had told me about his life. As a young boy, he was raised in church. Years down the road his mother was kicked to the side. There was something scandalous about it, and adding insult to injury no one would even answer him directly as to what was going on. It was a pretty detailed story that had some ugly twists all the way up to her death. He explained to me that's what had hurt him with church is how they treated his mother.

It was a distinct pleasure to lead our neighbor to the Lord and pray with him. This happened as he was on his deathbed. Knowing him, I saw his heart. He was a beautiful person inside; who'd been wounded by people that the Bible says will have a harsher judgment than he.

I've personally always hated labels and being marginalized. That is what people do though; that's why someone is either a woman preacher, or a black preacher. You never hear someone put an emphasis on a male clergyman. Is it possible in some cases that denoting someone as a woman preacher, or a black preacher is adding some sort of stigma to the term? In and of itself it seems like a means for concluding something. It's like saying that someone is a good preacher if they're well spoken, or that someone is a good-looking preacher if they're attractive to look at. Nobody that I've ever known expects a black preacher to be spiritually dried up. The stigmas with the black churches are that they're spiritual and vivacious. While there certainly is nothing wrong with being a woman, to some a woman preacher is a pejorative term. It's a strange line of thought as I've known some remarkably incompetent men who by hearing or observing them are a disservice to the church, yet I've observed them being promoted to the office of pastor.

In spite of this theologically flawed thinking, women have had a part in ministry during Old Testament times, even more heavily during the first century church, and have continued from there on.

Regarding, the Apostle Paul's discourse on church etiquette, in 1521AD Martin Luther wrote, "Order, good behaviour, honour, require that women should stop talking when a man speaks; but when no man speaks, women should preach." Nearly, two hundred and fifty years later the United States of America would be born, and not long after history would record the women preachers in this new land.

On February 11 1783, Jarena Lee was born. She came to know the Lord at a young age, and called by the Holy Spirit to preach. This was seemingly an exceptionally difficult task for a Negro woman in an era when slavery openly and lawfully existed, women could not vote, nor own land. She faced much bigotry and opposition both because she was a woman, and because she was black.

Jarena told Pastor Richard Allen of her calling, but due their organizations discriminatory attitude towards women within ministry she at that time was not permitted. Unwavering from her calling she later persisted until Richard Allen permitted her to have in home Bible studies, allowing her to expound on God's word, when it seemed appropriate. Due to the highly evident masochism that dominated the 19th century and Christian worldview, she was not permitted to preach her first sermon until 1817.

The evidence of calling was so overwhelming that Bishop Richard Allen then affirmed it. Jarena Lee was amidst the first female preachers within the United States. She held revival services from Maryland to Canada. Her autobiography records how in 1839 while holding a revival in Portsmouth, Ohio, five people fell out in the floor under the anointing of the Holy Spirit.

The fiery anointing upon Jarena Lee's ministry caused the AME to grow and flourish. Her biography was written as a defense of her calling to preach, as she felt it necessary to do so due to the woman-hating religious folks of that day who simply refused to believe that God would call a female into ministry in spite of the Bible's clarity showing how He did time and time again. She was laid to rest in 1864.

Given the name Isabella Baumfree at birth, history better knows this woman as Sojourner Truth. Born in 1797, she is listed within the Smithsonian's 100 Most Significant

Americans of all time. She was a traveling Methodist Preacher, who railed against the institution of slavery. Her most famous speech, which was written is southern slang was entitled, "Ain't I A Woman".

Sojourner's parents were bought at a slave auction, they lived in New York. When she was nine years old she was sold along with a flock of sheep for $100. At the time she only spoke Dutch. She'd have four different masters from that point on, the last of which was the kindest towards her, raped her, and thereby fathered her second child.

Her work as an evangelist began in 1843. She told her friends, "The Spirit calls me and I must go." She died in 1883. Sojourner Truth's life is remembered annually within both the Episcopal and Lutheran churches calendar of saints.

Phoebe Palmer was born to a New York family of devout Methodists in 1807. She felt conflicted over her peaceful relationship with God. She yearned for something more. After losing two young children and believing it punishment for not fully devoting herself to God, she came to "see that the error of my religious life has been a desire for signs and wonders. Like Naaman, I have wanted some great thing, unwilling to rely unwaveringly on the still small voice of the Spirit, speaking through the naked Word." She learned that by laying her life on the altar, she had full assurance of her salvation.

After this spiritual insight, she and her sister began holding ecumenical women's prayer meetings, which began to multiply into similar groups around the country.

Palmer became one of the most influential women in the fastest-growing religious group in America. She began to organize and preach at camp meetings, where approximately 25,000 people converted to Christianity. Her theology of the "altar covenant" was influential in the founding of the Church of the Nazarene, The Salvation Army, The Church of God, and The Pentecostal Holiness Church. Her book, The Way of Holiness was in fifty-two editions by 1867. She passed away in 1875.

Born in 1825, Antoinette Brown Blackwell was a precocious child living in Rochester, New York, who began preaching in her Congregational church at the age of nine. She was a schoolteacher for four years, saving money to enroll in Oberlin College, founded by Charles Finney and one of the first American colleges to train women in theology. Even so, her theology degree was withheld from her for several years due to discrimination against women in ministry.

Blackwell was a prolific writer and charismatic preacher. She eventually became the first woman to be ordained by a major American Protestant denomination in 1853. She continued preaching until 1915. Blackwell was also an abolitionist and early feminist, writing several books on women's rights and equality.

She was ordained by a church belonging to the Congregationalist Church. However, her ordination was not recognized by the denomination. Due to the bigotry, which she faced within the Congregationalist church for being a female minister, in 1878 Antoinette later resigned and became a Unitarian. The American Unitarian

Association wholeheartedly recognized her as a minister. Years later, the Congregationalists merged with others to create the United Church of Christ, which ordains women.

Amanda Berry Smith was born in 1837 to a Maryland slave who was able to buy his family's freedom. The Berry family resettled in Pennsylvania, where they became a station in the Underground Railroad. After becoming a Christian, she joined the African Methodist Episcopal Church. In 1869, she received her call to preach and over her career, became a popular speaker at churches and camp meetings from Maine to Tennessee. Smith was much loved for her beautiful singing voice and inspired sermons. She became the first black woman international evangelist in 1878, working in England, Ireland, Scotland, India and several African countries for twelve years. She died in 1915.

Though the course of time, God has called women to rise, making no distinction between male or female, Jew nor Greek, slave nor freeman. It's somewhat odd that individuals professing to know scripture will proclaim that God wouldn't call a woman into ministry like He would a man because scripture teaches that the woman is the weaker vessel. (1st Peter 3:7) It's odd because if anything that'd be an evident point as to God's openness to use women within ministry. Scripture teaches that God's strength is made perfect through our weakness.

Scholars and philosophers have looked at the Bible and viewed God's choosing. How is it that God didn't choose Rome or Babylon, which were both some great things, but rather God chose the Jewish people? Military experts agree that facing the insurmountable odds that they've faced, that the victories that the Jewish people have won would be a complete impossibility in the natural. In the Bible we find God selecting Gideon who was a part of the smallest clan within the smallest tribe of Israel. If God was looking to pick the weakest vessel, it looked like He'd done it. Then he used Gideon to attain the victory over the enemy.

God chose David, a man after his own heart to be the king over Israel while David was a boy. Wasn't David the perceivably the weakest vessel in his father Jesse's household? When the prophet came to anoint one of Jesse's sons as king over all of Israel they were all there, except for David. Jesse saw David as unimportant, insignificant, and unworthy. In spite of Jesse's judgment, God spoke to Samuel instructing him not to look at the outside of the person, but to judge with righteous judgment as He does, looking within.

In regard to this, the tragedy is that supposedly righteous people are still judging others based on the color of their skin, the clothes they wear, and frankly their genitalia. Religiosity coupled with flawed perspective on scriptural truth says to the woman solely because she is a woman, "God wouldn't call someone like you." Sadly, in oppressing or suppressing someone whom God has legitimately called, we're not just working against that individual person, we're fighting against God himself.

A person can be sincere in their beliefs, and likewise they can be sincerely wrong. The bullheadedness of people when you point to them innumerate examples of God utilizing women in fundamental roles thought history is reminiscent of talking to a wall. They'll believe what they believe and do what they do. The belief that a woman isn't fit for some level of ministry merely because she is female doesn't necessarily make someone a bad person; it just makes him or her wrong.

Jesus Christ's confidence in women was so great that he entrusted women with the story of the resurrection, on which the entirety of the Gospel message hangs. He sought out a woman at a well who had been thrown away by every man she'd ever know. Looking for a man who would love and accept her just as she was, in walks that man Jesus. After their conversation, and her conversion, we see that she; a woman becomes the first missionary to spread the news of Jesus Christ to the Samaritan people.

Before Jesus died, a woman came to him with a box of expensive perfume. History teaches us that this perfume would have cost one year's wages. With His disciples present she entered the room where they were. She began to anoint Jesus Christ with that perfume. She washed his feet with her tears and dried them with her hair. Making one of the greatest statements that has ever been made, Christ told her that wherever this Gospel is told, that what she had done on that day would be told too.

In the Proverbs, the Christ-like character of wisdom is rightfully defined as being a woman, as the word for wisdom (חָכְמוֹת - ḥā-ḵə-mō-wṯ) is feminine in nature. In life, we find that it's not women that struggle associating emotion with thought, but rather it's men. I'd heard one preacher exclaim, "That if we men are just as much a part of the bride of Christ as women are, then women are just as much sons of God as us."

Since the times of the nineteen hundreds, the realization as to God's apparent callings placed upon the lives of women has become more prominent. With the rise of pastors like Amy Semple McPherson who worked exhaustively within ministry, fed over 5 million people during the great depression, and founded the Four Square Church organization to clergy like Elisabeth Elliot who famously won a tribe of savage natives to the Lord Jesus Christ after that massacred her husband. Elisabeth became a world-renowned author, radio host, missionary, and professor, inspiring countless numbers of people within ministry and Christendom. And while in the twenty-first century women within ministry is relatively common, there is still overwhelming resistance and sanctimonious hatred directed towards them.

Charles Spurgeon famously said, "Discernment is not a matter of telling the difference between right and wrong; rather it is telling the difference between right and almost right." Self-righteousness looks a lot like righteousness. It's easy to take a passage here and a passage there out of the Bible and mangle God's perfect word into saying whatever suits you. It's sad that when you talk about what a Greek word means that in their ignorance some people just blow that off. It's a certainty that some "Christians" are so stupid that they honestly believe when the Apostle Paul was preaching he was preaching from the King James Bible. I once even spoke with a very enthusiastic devout Baptist who exclaimed boastfully, "John was a Baptist!"

The sole reason that there wasn't an epistle to the Berea Church is because they studied out the scriptures. As a pastor and theologian, it pains me how the average churchgoer doesn't know rudimentary subjects and stories within the Bible. It pains me how there are teachers put over youth who themselves are unteachable, or unwilling to learn. It pains me when a man is moved forward and a woman is held back on the basis of their gender.

CHAPTER 7: DIVORCE IS DIVORCE OF COURSE; OF COURSE?

In regard to the qualifications of a Bishop: which is an administrative overseer, and likewise the qualifications a deacon: who ministers to the widow and orphans, cleans the church, mows the lawn, and otherwise is the established servant role of the church, we find them in 1st Timothy 3 which reads as follows:

Qualifications for Overseers/Bishops (1st Timothy 3:1-7)

"This is a true saying, If a man desire the office of a bishop, he desireth a good work. A bishop then must

be blameless, the husband of one wife, vigilant, sober, of good behaviour, given to hospitality, apt to teach; Not given to wine, no striker, not greedy of filthy lucre; but patient, not a brawler, not covetous; One that ruleth well his own house, having his children in subjection with all gravity;(For if a man know not how to rule his own house, how shall he take care of the church of God?) Not a novice, lest being lifted up with pride he fall into the condemnation of the devil. Moreover, he must have a good report of them which are without; lest he fall into reproach and the snare of the devil."

Qualifications for Deacons (1st Timothy 3:8-13)

"Likewise must the deacons be grave, not double-tongued, not given to much wine, not greedy of filthy lucre; Holding the mystery of the faith in a pure conscience. And let these also first be proved; then let them use the office of a deacon, being found blameless. Even so must their wives be grave, not slanderers, sober, faithful in all things. Let the deacons be the husbands of one wife, ruling their children and their own houses well. For they that have used the office of a deacon well purchase to themselves a good degree, and great boldness in the faith which is in Christ Jesus."

An individual could easily go off into a male chauvinistic rant about how a deacon is a male role. However, as we've previously discussed; Phoebe is listed as a deacon in the New Testament. There are historical references of the existence of deaconesses within the early church. The same exact Greek word was equally applied to both male deacons and female deaconesses up until the Council of Nicea, who amongst many other things, made a differentiation; applying a feminized term to the female deacons. It's quite clear due to the empirical evidence that the role of a deacon (i.e. servant) is gender neutral.

Many have concluded that because of an egalitarianism of the office of deacon, that the office of an Overseer/Bishop holds the same neutrality between the sexes. This is only further justified when noting that 2nd John is written to an Elect Elder Woman of the church, that Deborah was called of God to be a Judge over Israel, and so forth. Beyond these points, there's another group of people which are inappropriately cast aside by those taking 1st Timothy 3:1-13 out of context.

To many there is a cryptic message damning anyone who has been divorced at any time, for any reason. There are a myriad of problems with that. First, Divorce is not exclusively the issue that is being talked about. Secondly, just because someone gets a divorce doesn't necessarily mean that they've sinned by doing so. Thirdly, just because someone sins it doesn't mean that they're perpetually living in a state of unforgivable sin for the rest of their life as a result of poor decisions from their past.

I've had people ask me before, "Why is the God of the New Testament so different from the God of the Old Testament?" It's a question that illustrates that the person asking doesn't understand the Old Testament. The mercies of God searched a corrupt world over, which was plagued with evil and the hybrid giant children of human beings and fallen angels called the nephilim to find one man (Noah) and his family whom through them He saved the human race. God in his mercy would spare the entire valley of Sodom and Gomorrah if he found ten people who were not wholly wicked there. Upon finding that there were not the small number of 10 people in this huge area, which did not deserve execution for their vast evil, two angels were sent as messengers to tell Lot, a righteous man; who he and his family were still tainted by this society. In their escape, amidst all of the other dramatic events surrounding this; Lot asked God to spare a small town in the area for his sake so he could live there. God did. Scientists feel that the destruction of the valley of Sodom and Gomorrah was executed by way of a volcanic eruption, which could easily correspond with what the Bible describes. These are but a few of many accounts in the Old Testament where the mercies of God are displayed. God's mercy is a consistent pattern. David wrote about God's mercy in Psalms, Jeremiah in Lamentation chapter 3, and so forth. Doesn't it seem that people read 1st Timothy 3:1-13 through a flawed lens?

The emphasis to be made in regard to what the qualification of a Bishop or Overseer is: "Moreover he must have a good report of them which are without; lest he fall into reproach and the snare of the devil." Every single thing mentioned about someone's character is talking about how they are now. According to the Bible bishop must be of good behavior. On that one case alone, if we were to say that someone would have always been of good behavior, then no one would be qualified. A bishop must be patient. Again, if we looked at that thinking it meant that a person must have always had to be patient, no one would be qualified. Often times the same law that people use to condemn others just spins back around and damns themselves due to their own gross inadequacy.

Regarding the phrasing "husband of one wife", what it's saying in the literal Greek is a "One woman man". There are a lot of men who have been married for year, never divorced, and they're not a one-woman man. You know the type. Their eye wanders. They're caught up in lust. Some even commit marital infidelity, which in the Old Testament would have resulted in public shame and execution. Still, overtime these people have been permitted to hold the highest offices in the house of God, while others are excluded for what sanctimonious men have governed as the unpardonable sin of divorce. It's an extraordinarily odd thing too, seeing as how there are several circumstances where the Bible allows provision for people to get divorced.

By Old Testament standards divorcing someone for the act of adultery, and remarrying would be a non-issue. This is because, as opposed to fornication, which suffered the penalty of scourging, adultery was so heinous of a crime that it resulted in public shame and execution by being publicly stoned to death. That was the pattern of what happened all the way up to the book of Hosea, where a prophet gave mercy to his unfaithful wife.

The clear question in that specific circumstance is, "Whereas the adulterous sinner is shown mercy (not killed) should the victim be made to suffer?" It'd sound monstrous to even consider answering that with a yes. Sadly, many churches have taken that exact stance on that exact issue. It's Godless treachery like this that causes the on-looking world to say, "Christians are the only army that shoot their wounded."

Simply put, victimizing a victim of adultery, abuse, abandonment, and divorce, who is faithful doesn't make you like Jesus, it makes you like the Pharisee that stepped to the other side of the road letting the beaten man die of his wounds. There are some really evil biases out there towards both women and divorcees. It's purely evil when a woman is forcibly raped for a person to ask what she was wearing or to infer that she somehow caused it. Yet the pious judgments held so dear by many misconstrue the Bible in the way they've heard it taught, or the way that simply suits them best.

In Jesus time, there were two schools of Jewish teaching; the school of Hillel and the School of Shammai. While both differed in opinion over a multiplicity of subjects, what they did agree upon was that there were causes acceptable for divorce. Hillel taught that a man could divorce his wife for any imaginable reason. Shammai taught that divorce was only permitted via conditions stated within scripture.

Inside proper hermeneutical study, you'd start with torah; the first five books of the Bible. The Old Testament prophets then expounded upon them, and the New Testament then expounds all of that. This is why when Jesus was asked about divorce, He directed them back to the torah (i.e. the law given down by God through Moses). The scripture that Jesus was speaking of says: "When a man hath taken a wife, and married her, and it come to pass that she find no favour in his eyes, because he hath found some uncleanness in her: then let him write her a bill of divorcement, and give it in her hand, and send her out of his house." (Deuteronomy 24:1)

Yet, in spite of this we still face a society that mutilates the truth of scripture, condemning others while exalting themselves. Much like the verses afore mentioned within 1st Timothy 2 and 1st Corinthians 14 which are utilized by misogynistic to defame women, sanctimonious people are also quick to exclaimed, "God hates divorce." For what it's worth, the Bible does have God saying that He hates divorce. That however is not to say that He hates divorced people, or that He did not allow conditions for divorce. The verse they're referencing says: "For the LORD, the God of Israel, saith that he hateth putting away: for one covereth violence with his garment, saith the LORD of hosts: therefore take heed to your spirit, that ye deal not treacherously." (Malachi 2:16)

The tragedy is that by stripping one line out of the Bible, it can often be misused and lose its context. Such is the case with "Judge Not". It's a popular quote from where Jesus was telling people how to judge righteously and without hypocrisy. He followed in explaining first deal with yourself, and then you'll be able to help some-

one else afflicted with the same problem. He empha-
sized the importance of exercising good judgment in
saying, "Can the blind lead the blind? Won't they both
fall into a ditch?" Just as bad as ripping "judge not" from
a sermon on using good judgment is people ripping
"God hates divorce" from the Bible and twisting it in a
way that hurts people.

Yes, God hates divorce. Many divorced people
hate divorce. Sometimes life doesn't offer us any easy
choices. Just because someone divorces it doesn't
mean they've done something wrong. Does the Bible
teach that? Yes, God divorced Israel. The Bible says: "The
LORD said also unto me in the days of Josiah the king,
Hast thou seen that which backsliding Israel hath done?
she is gone up upon every high mountain and under
every green tree, and there hath played the harlot. And I
said after she had done all these things, Turn thou unto
me. But she returned not. And her treacherous sister Judah saw it. And I saw, when for all the causes whereby
backsliding Israel committed adultery I had put her
away, and given her a bill of divorce; yet her treacherous sister Judah feared not, but went and played the
harlot also." (Jeremiah 3:6-8)

In the Old Testament time, the people of God had
transgressed by marrying pagan foreigners. With repentance in their hearts they asked God to forgive them,
and seeking to right their wrongs they divorced their
wives. Scripture says: "Now when Ezra had prayed, and
when he had confessed, weeping and casting himself
down before the house of God, there assembled unto
him out of Israel a very great congregation of men and

women and children: for the people wept very sore. And Shechaniah the son of Jehiel, one of the sons of Elam, answered and said unto Ezra, we have trespassed against our God, and have taken strange wives of the people of the land: yet now there is hope in Israel concerning this thing. 3 Now therefore let us make a covenant with our God to put away all the wives, and such as are born of them, according to the counsel of my lord, and of those that tremble at the commandment of our God; and let it be done according to the law. Arise; for this matter belongeth unto thee: we also will be with thee: be of good courage, and do it. (Ezra 10:1-4)

It's clear that in the book of Ezra that the worst thing wasn't getting divorced, but being unequally yoked; marrying pagans and adopting their ways. In the book of Jeremiah it's apparent that God has not transgressed against the nation of Israel who had whored itself with other deities, finally causing God to divorce Himself from her. Divorce doesn't equate to sin. Unfortunately, sometimes a divorce is the only valid response to marital circumstances that we face in this fallen world.

God does not instruct someone to stay married in cases of abandonment. Regarding this, the Apostle Paul writes: "But if the unbelieving depart, let him depart. A brother or a sister is not under bondage in such cases: but God hath called us to peace." (1st Corinthians 7:15) Perhaps that's somewhat of a deep issue, as there is a physical and emotional abandonment. Reconciliation is the course that we all should pursue within marriage if possible. The truth is, that you can't make people change. Hence, we have the example where God felt forced into divorcing Israel.

God's plan from the very beginning was for one man and one woman to be united in marriage. However, due to circumstances within the Old Testament and the mercies of God, He did allow for some things to go on. While I'm not building a case for polygamy or concubines, I am mentioning that this was the distinct context of the verses that I'm about to reference. The law given within them break down the responsibilities of the husband within a marriage, and how they were not to diminish towards the woman who was the wife on the side. All women deserved far better than to be treated like they're second-class. Those verses read: "If he take him another wife; her food, her raiment, and her duty of marriage, shall he not diminish. And if he do not these three unto her, then shall she go out free without money." (Exodus 21:10-11)

It is important to note that Exodus 21:10-11 is outlining that a man's responsibility in marriage is to provide 3 things to his wife. Those three things are: food, clothing, and love. According to the Bible if the husband neglects his wife, she is free to divorce him. A neglectful husband is not only a failure as a husband, but a failure as a man (1st Timothy 5:8).

God's will is not for someone to be trapped in a Godless marriage that was painted like one thing, and then turned out to be another. God doesn't want someone trapped in a relationship filled with abuse, degradation, infidelity, or abandonment. We are called into holiness and faithfulness by a God that loves.

Jesus Christ himself recognized there were conditions where divorce is the only viable option. Though in understanding what he said and what Deuteronomy 24:1 says, which he was siting, only expands upon the appropriate circumstances for divorce that he mentioned. In the King James Bible the translation from the Hebrew word (עֶרְוַת - 'er-waṯ) that is "uncleanness" can also be translated "indecency", "nakedness", and an array of terms. While the meaning is clear, it is equally a bit broad perspectively allowing room for something less precise than sexual intercourse. After all, if a married person were having sexual intercourse with someone else, that'd be adultery. This is why Jesus used two different Greek words in saying: "It hath been said, whosoever shall put away his wife, let him give her a writing of divorcement: But I say unto you, That whosoever shall put away his wife, saving for the cause of fornication, causeth her to commit adultery: and whosoever shall marry her that is divorced committeth adultery." (Matthew 5:31-32)

The Greek word, which is translated into adultery exclusively, means adultery. However, the word used for fornication has a broader meaning; that word is "porneia". It's the root term for the English terms pornography and pornographic. It's derived from the Greek word "pernaō" which means to sell off. Essentially, it's the selling off or surrendering of sexual purity via promiscuity of any and/or every type.

Because of God's allowances for divorce under certain situation, it'd be unthinkable to logically determine that the context of the qualifications for a deacon and bishop are meant to rail against a faithful person who due to circumstance had to get a divorce in their past, yet people think it.

Due to the Apostle Paul listing Phoebe as a deacon, and church history validating that there were deaconesses within the church body until the Catholic church elected to take bigoted stances against women, we know that 1st Timothy chapter 3's qualifications for such must have been received as gender neutral. It was the same Apostle Paul that worked alongside women regarding them equally to his brothers as laborers in Christ. It was the Apostle Paul who wrote: "There is neither Jew nor Greek, there is neither bond nor free, there is neither male nor female: for ye are all one in Christ Jesus." (Galatians 3:28)

In stark contrast to religious society and man-made oral traditions God's holy word has never sought to call the equipped, but rather to equip the called. It has not been God who has brought up peoples past repentant sins, but the work of Satan. I've explained to people that repentance isn't when you cry; it's when you change. As teachers, we're held more accountable than those who are not. (James 3:1)

The qualifications of a Bishop and Deacon are about examining someone's character in the present. Essentially, it's asking the church to determine if the candidate is a model Christian of upstanding reputation, whether they are a man or woman.

EPILOGUE

In a speech given on the subject of misogyny in church, Pastor Eugene Cho explained that in Korea married women traditionally would not take their husband's last name. He stated that it wasn't because of equality, but rather because they were unworthy. He also added that it has been common for a woman to walk at least three steps behind her husband due to her perceived inferiority, whereas she is female. As awful as that sounds, religious men have often mangled the Bible by using it as an attack on women.

Simply to rehash what we've already discussed I would state, in the second chapter of Genesis we read the account where God creates woman. Kindly, God states that he'll make Adam a "helper". It's a highly positive term that Godless stupidity has put an ugly tone to. This word that was used to identify Eve's role in relation to her husband Adam is also used multiple times in the Bible to describe God.

Eve was not Adam's inferior who should be lagging behind him, or placed under him. Rather, what the term "helper" would suggest is that she was at his side working and fighting along with him. Eve was Adam's wife, collaborator, and friend. They walked together in unity.

Perhaps one of the more concerning issues regarding women or divorcees within ministry is the callousness displayed by much of the pious religious community in being open to what the Bible actually says. It's self-defeating to claim that you believe that the Bible is the infallible inspired word of God, and then reject the fullness of scripture. In an interview via a podcast that is produced by Fuller Theological Seminary, Rev. Beth Moore expressed that she does not have a problem with people teaching 1st Timothy 2 and 1st Corinthians 14. She then added that she has a problem when that's all that someone teaches. Rev. Moore says she has always particularly been called to minister to women. She's been ridiculed by a number of male clergymen throughout her ministry for being a woman preacher.

How long will supposed Christian leadership claiming to be ordained of God and presuming to be studied in scripture continue to abuse people in the name of the Lord Jesus Christ? It's quite certain that people can be wrong about things and still be a Christian. Everything is not a salvation issue. Clearly, there are people that I can reach that other Christians can't, while at the same time, there are people that others can reach that I can't. What if a woman is whom God chooses? What if it's a woman like the woman at the well who essentially became the first evangelist to the Samaritan people? In the 21st century there are underground Christian movements going across the Middle Eastern world, many of which are being led by women. There are women standing up for the Gospel of Jesus Christ in the most hostile environments to women and Christians alike. I'm fully convinced because of the Bible that these women are just as called of God as any man.

Consistently, the choosing of the Lord is completely out of sorts with who man would choose. In the book of Judges God chose Jephthah the Gileadite, the son of a prostitute, perceivably during an extramarital affair, to lead the Israelites to victory. Thrown away like a piece of garbage due to the nature of his birth, our loving God chose to work through him. Time and time again in scripture we see that God chose the underdogs, many of which were women to rise to the occasion and bring glory to His name, and victory to His people.

The story of Ester really begins from a story within the life of King Saul. During his reign, Saul had received a command from the Lord to completely lay waste to the Amalekites. He was to kill every man, woman, child, and animal. Not adhering to God's command, Saul let their king, Agog as well as the sheep and oxen live. As usual, God was right in telling Saul to kill every last one. If Saul had done as the Lord asked then not only would God not have departed from him, but the wicked genocidal maniac Haman of the book of Ester would not have been born, as he was a descendent of King Agog. Given

Hamon's family history, this wicked man had an en-grained bitterness for the Jewish people. God's response was to take a Hebrew girl and elevate her to greatness as a Persian Queen to bring this evil man down.

Remember, Hagar the bondservant of Sarah, and her son Ishmael were cast out from the camp. Essentially, Abraham divorced her. As she had run out of water, and wept there in the desert praying for God not to let her see the death of her son, the Lord spoke to her from Heaven promising to bless her child and raise up a great nation from him. Their story is a difficult thing. The favor of God was with them. We also see Biblical evidence that Abraham had an ongoing relationship with his son Ish-mael to whatever extent. Both Isaac and Ishmael were together to bury their father when he died.

In the non-canonical book of Jasher, or more specifically what's claimed to be the book of Jasher, there is an account where Abraham rides a camel to pay a visit to his grown married son Ishmael. The story tells that he has a jerk wife, who trash talks him to this stranger; that she doesn't realize is his Dad. Abraham gives her a veiled message to repeat. Ishmael under-stands the message is that his Dad visited and how his wife acted, and he needs to divorce her, so he does. Some years later, according to the story Abraham sets out on a camel again. This time, Ishmael has a sweet lov-ing, kind wife. She offers Abraham sustenance, speaks well of her husband, who like the time before is on a hunting trip. A veiled message again is left to be relayed to his son, Ishmael, this time the message was that he married well and to hang on to her. Whether the occurrence within the professed book of Jasher is correct or not, we do have every reason to believe that Abraham loved all of his children deeply.

Over and over again God has chosen the individuals that people overlooked, underrated, discounted, or dismissed to be utilized for His glorious kingdom. Neither the divorced, nor the poor, nor the broken, nor the women, nor the disabled are discounted by the Lord. God honors faithfulness. Just because someone is divorced doesn't mean they've sinned. Just because something terrible has happened in someone's distant past doesn't mean it should necessarily mark his or her future.

I personally hate being marginalized. Marginalization is bigotry. Claiming that every woman is this way, or every black person is that way, or every divorcee without exclusion has perpetuated sin when the Bible honestly teaches otherwise is a wildly bigoted worldview. To those professing to be Christians I would admonish you that you actually need to strive to be Christ-like, operating in the fullness of God's word and not disproportionately taking scripture out of context.

It is my sincere hope that this book has opened each reader's eyes to what the Bible says on this topic. When discussing women's roles within ministry Dr. Michael Heiser has given a lot of valuable insights. Being a real scholar, he's presented a wealth of academic arguments from individuals on both side of the issue. He's added that he could personally argue either side quite well; stating that if his daughter felt called of the Lord he'd tell her that is between her and God, because at the end of it that's what really matters. Regarding his willingness to teach on the subject he stated, "It's not a hill to die on." The question in relevance to this is: if you as a Christian leader are suppressing the people who God has called, are you not fighting against God himself and perpetuating evil through ignorance, piousness, bigotry, or by whatever means? These are all questions worth asking and things to think upon.

Thank you for taking the time to read this book. I sincerely hope it has a positive effect on your life, and walk for God. The will of the Lord is neither to suppress people nor to make them change per say. It's to call them back, to bring them home, hence the term repentance. From the fall of man, the entirety of scripture has been about restoring the perfect Edenic conditions we mankind had cast aside via sin.

As a means of closing out this book, I feel it appropriate to end with a prayer.

Gracious Heavenly Father, who made all things perfect and created all of mankind and womankind in your divine image, we thank you for filling us with the breath of life, which came directly from you. We thank you for the inherent value that this gives all of us. We thank you that your word doesn't condone racism nor gender abuse, but it continually tears it down. We thank you that even in times when people who loved you were downcast, that in your sovereign grace and mercy, you've elected to elevate whom you wish in spite of the flawed and often bigoted perspectives of people.

Jesus, never has there been a person like you. None have had such compassion on sinners and broken people. We thank you that in knowing all things, being fully God and fully man, seeing us at our very worst, that you'd rather die than to live without us. We thank you the Gospel clearly shows your heart in saying that you had to go through Samaria, where you saved that poor broken woman's soul. Help us to be more like you and to operate in the perfect truth of The Word, rather than slanted perspectives and traditions of men.

Sweet Holy Spirit, we ask that you'd temper us on both a conscious and unconscious level with an overflowing fullness of the attributes regarded within what scripture refers to as the fruit of the Spirit. Fill us with the perfect love of God, which preexists all creation. Fill us with joy even in the trying and disagreeable times in life. Give us a peace that is grounded in you, and not contingent on the circumstances or metaphorical storms that surround us. Envelop my very being with a grace and kindness that precludes from being spiritually damaging the frail and weak of faith and mind. Encompass me with your goodness so that I can be like you, act like you, speak like you, listen and understand like you. Let longsuffering and gentleness be conjoined to my nature. Allow me the faith to trust in you, your will, your way, and your word fully; and not place it in uncertain things. Bless me with an overwhelming abundance of self-control, removing any level spiritual or psychological myopathy allowing my foresight to be a highly attuned as my hindsight.

God, yours is the kingdom, and the glory, and the power forever. Amen.

THANK FOR WOMEN PREACHERS' POST SCRIPT

Well, congratulations! You made it through the book. As I was studying up on the sections that make up a book, I found that there is this magical thing called the postscript, as in PS. This not only helps add a few more pages to the book to prevent any detractors from mocking it for being a light read; it also allows me to do what we preachers love best, rabbit-trail after side subjects which would've run the chapters off the rails if it was done inside of them!

If you'd like to keep reading, think of this as that special time when they show clips during the credits at the end of movies. In this section, I'll be sharing side stories, and information that is not mildly associated with, but not directly relevant to the primary content that's been discussed. What I'm going to try to do somewhat is keep the side content in the order of the chapters, more or less. Just don't hold me to it though. And again, thank you for reading this book.

INTRODUCTION POST SCRIPT

Each time I'd sit down to write this book I would pray intently for the guidance of the Holy Spirit. I realized that the subject matter within it goes against some people's doctrinal grain. As it's been mentioned several times within the book, which of itself shines like a hot neon light piercing through still blackest night; only serving to illuminate there are deeply ingrained problems that have infected people's minds within the church construct like a pandemic.

The plain simple truth is that we can be unified without uniformity. There will be Baptists, Pentecostals, Methodists, Presbyterians, and an array of people from within different denominations and doctrines who will be in Heaven. In the third chapter of Revelation, the Apostle John wrote a letter as it was dictated to him by the Spirit of Jesus Christ. Specifically, I'm referring to the church of Sardis. Their condemnation was that they had a good name, which meant they were alive, but in fact they were dead. Amidst the laundry list as to how bad they are, the letter tells us that there were still some who had not defiled their garments.

Scripturally speaking there are people that are saved even within dead churches. There are a wealth of things that we can be wrong about and still be saved. The sadness is how through arrogance or some other reasoning, many people tend become defensive who say they believe what the Bible teaches, at the very mention of examining that what they feel the Bible teaches might be misjudgment.

If you've read this book and find yourself getting bent out of shape over its content which expresses that God doesn't differentiate men and women within ministry like many organized churches do, I think it'd be productive if you take the time to sincerely ask yourself why that is. I mean, if it angers you to hear another point of view, which is derived from the fullness of scripture, why? I would thoroughly enjoy conversing with anyone who sincerely wanted to politely have a discussion regarding the matter.

Sometimes some people's reaction to statements or events says more about them that the statements or events. Frankly, there are a lot of preachers I could've named by name and told some short pithy stories about, yet I've kept them at a minimum and elected not to name any a great deal of names. ...for now anyway.

CHAPTER 1 POST SCRIPT

In the first chapter, I began by telling a story to set the tone. Unfortunately, there have been a great deal of times when I've been in the church house and it's not been in decency and order. As a young man I visited a singing at one super trashy country storefront church where two poorly groomed medium-sized dogs, potentially with fleas, were running loose in the room used for that church's sanctuary while a singing was going on. If that weren't bad enough someone then dashed out from the kitchen with a small dog-carrying cage under his or her arm. The small dog was barking and making an awful racket. The smell hit you in the face that it'd apparently defecated all in the cage, and they were abruptly rushing it out of the church.

At another small backwoods church, I was sitting on the back pew with my family. As a teenage preacher, I used to comb my hair back like Elvis Presley or Conway Twitty and over dress for everything. There I was looking sharp as could be when this eight to twelve-year-old child turned around and stared at me like they were mesmerized. Finally, the kid, who was acting as if they an extra from the movie Deliverance or Wrong Turn looked over at my Mom and asked the question, perpetually in slow motion, regarding myself, "Is she a boy?" My Mom and Grandma just about fell out of the pew they laughed so hard amidst the stupidity. I just looked disgusted over the whole thing. I guess the kid thought I was pretty or something, but really, what kinda question is that anyway?

I have had one church bass player tell me all you have to do to play the bass guitar is play one string; which speaks of his level of quality, or the lack there of. At eighteen years old, I was cornered by a drug addict woman outside of the church I attended whose age was indiscernible, as she looked so rough. As a young preacher, I made it a habit to sit on the front row, and pray with people in the altar. At eighteen I looked like I was about fourteen or fifteen. I was tall, pale, thin, freckle faced, with very big hair, and glasses. As I finished praying for that particular woman, she asked could she talk to me in private. I accommodated her request.

We stepped out the churches front door. The strange woman asked, "Do I know you from somewhere?" Honestly, I can tell you I would have remembered her if we had. She was very distinctive looking. She had a Bart Simpson haircut and sores on her face. Her teeth had been eaten away by meth, and her gums were the poster child for pyorrhea. She was wearing a stained shirt and sweatpants that were cut off to the knees. The pants also looked dingy. At that time in my life, I wanted to grow a beard, but couldn't. She had more facial hair than I did. And there I was, a naive young boy being kind to her.

I answered her question about whether we'd met before or not, unaware that she was trying to pursue some sort of romantic relationship with me. My dialog turned into me honestly stating where I'd worked in the area, how I'd went out with my local church going door to door witnessing, etc. Finally, she just came out, cut through all the garbage, and asked if she'd have a chance with me. I stuttered and stammered, saying how I was interested in someone else, trying to let her down as easy as I could. It seemed like I was suspended in time. Then the church doors opened, and she seemed to disappear. Once I got in my family's car, I told them what happened and my little old grandma wanted to whoop her!

I've known of trashy little churches in run-down buildings where everyone and their cousin were let up to sing, who couldn't carry a tune in a bucket. They'd nearly all feel to sing two to five songs each. The pastor would excuse it saying if he didn't let these people be used in doing something they obviously had no calling to do, then no one would come to their church. At that same church, which has now been closed for years, drug deals would go down in the parking lot during service. At another church over 700 miles away and at least a decade before, they'd lob a roll of French bread around the room for Holy Communion, having people tear a piece off when it came to them. During one service, that same pastor was walking around in a long robe saying whoever touched the hem of his garment would be healed.

Needless to say, every single one of those churches was lead by men. There was not one woman deacon, nor one woman on the board. Sadly by virtue of these pastors being male, some people would be so misguided to think they're more qualified than any female. It's point that is clearly wrong.

A woman I know, whom I have an abundance of confidence in: told me a story of how she was attending a particular Baptist church years ago. They were small and had no sort of youth program. She took it on and built one from the ground up. Once it had become sizable, the local church board called a meeting and removed her from the position of being a youth leader there, because she's a woman.

I've known of some really awful things happening in church, whether it was in the name of the Lord or other sorts of misconduct. The church had always been my happy place growing up. I was bullied terribly as a child.

I've endured a lot of abuse of various sorts. Because of it all, I've had a lot of anger and pain. The church has always been my soft place to land, even though during my late teens through my early thirties, I'd be wounded by church people over and over again.

God has been good to me. We as the church need to come together, work together, strive together with our fellow brothers and sisters alike in the faith. There were a lot of questions that were asked in the first chapter, and really that's part of what good Bible study is. A productive Bible study is often comprised of asking questions and saturating yourself with knowledge and scripture on that subject, which can lead to other questions and rabbit trail you all over that area.

CHAPTER 2 POST SCRIPT

In the second chapter of this book, we discussed Jesus Christ's love and egalitarian attitude towards women. An act of love for His mother Mary, Jesus instructs the Apostle John to take care of her. Notably John did. Mary's last home was in Ephesus. The location where it is said to be can be toured today, if you're ever in Turkey.

Oddly, a story that Mary the Mother of Jesus makes me think of is Queen Mary aka Bloody Mary, the Queen of England. She was the bastard daughter of Henry VIII. The Anglican Church was founded as it broke away from the Roman Catholic Church so that Henry could divorce Mary's mother, and thereby marry a his next wife, who bore their daughter Elizabeth.

Queen Mary, after she eventually took the throne, was a Christian killing genocidal lunatic and devout Catholic. When the Pope came to visit and greeted her with the words, "Blessed art thou Mary, and highly favored amongst women." She convinced herself that it was a message from God that like Mary the mother of Jesus, she too would conceive a child. After a false pregnancy and locking herself away for twelve months she came back as the historical Christian burning monster of which legend speaks. The next queen would be Queen Elizabeth who had been imprisoned in a tower by her half-sister Bloody Mary. ...How's that for a rabbit trail?

The Mary of the Bible not only delivered the Son of God, Yeshua (Jesus) the Messiah, she was also a disciple of Christ, she was at the cross, but she was also in the upper room and received the infilling of the Holy Ghost at Pentecost. In the non-canonical book entitled "The Protoevangelium of James", the story of Mary begins as one of the faithful of God chosen to take part in making the veil for the Holiest of Holies. Whether that account is true or not, she certainly was pure, faithful and chosen of God.

CHAPTER 3 POST SCRIPT

As mentioned previously in this book, the city of Ephesus was associated with the Amazon warrior women of Greek mythology. Just like the giant squid and silver back gorilla, people assumed it was just a myth too and were proved wrong. Archeological digs have found the graves of female warriors in regions near what is now Mongolia.

In other areas across the Angolan region there have been found tribal people groups where the men and women would go into battle and into the hunt together. The overly inflated lore created surrounding the Amazon women within Greek mythology was a way of demonizing an enemy and making the heroes which conquered them seem all the greater.

As millennia would pass, books were written by people still fascinated by the subject. The Amazon River in South America was named after the Amazons. Sailors traveling it in search of the lost treasure of the Amazons claimed to see Amazonian female warriors standing along the edges of the river. Whereas the native men in this region of the world don't have hairy chests and have long hair, it's been questioned whether the sailors saw female warriors at all.

The state of California was likewise named after the Amazons of myth. The state is specifically named after one of the Amazons queens. Her name was Calafia. However, she is not out of Greek myth, but rather a fictional creation of writer Garci Rodríguez de Montalvo, from his book "The Adventures of Esplandián", which was written around 1500. History records that the sailors claimed to have seen Amazon women adorned with golden armor there in the Golden State.

In the Parthenon, Amazon women were painted upon its pillars. Children played with Amazon dolls. Pottery was often painted with Amazon women. The Ephesian people lived in a society that thought of menstrual blood as sacred. Ephesus was a vast metropolis centered around Goddess worship and the divine feminine. Dr. Carla Lonescu, a scholar whose studies revolve around Goddess worship and the divine feminine, put Artemis of the Ephesians in a special categorization. She stated that Artemis was made of dark stone, which only happens with several other female deities. The assertion is that they are considered mother-creator. Whether it's true or not, as a scholar and expert in her field she further asserts that the Catholic church has utilized syncretism to rebrand the Goddess Artemis as the Virgin Mary, whom is also rendered in black/burnt stone. This was all part of her dissertation entitled, "THE ENDURING GODDESS: Artemis and Mary, Mother of Jesus."

The term Amazon actually means "one breasted" according to legend the Amazonian women would sever one of their breasts to become more effective with a bow. They have been portrayed as everything between bloodthirsty savages to nymphomaniacs. Greek writers like Plato, Strabo, and Herodotus all fully believed that these warrior women existed. Within Greek art the earliest portrayals of these women were in Greek art portrayed as wearing Greek armor and with Greek weapons. Later they were shown wearing clothing which was historically found by Scythian warriors. Archeologists have found that the Scythian people trained both males and females to ride horses and fight as archers.

CHAPTER 5 POST SCRIPT

There are a small number of women from the Bible period who I did not mention. History records that during the second century Beruriah was not only the wife of a sage, but an equally great sage, and a female rabbi. Within the Christendom there has obviously been a larger number of women in ministry through the progression of time. This started with Jesus Christ himself instituting and calling women into evangelistic and disciple roles within the Gospels. God's view of equality, echoing back from the prophecy of Joel was only further propelled at Pentecost.

CHAPTER 6 POST SCRIPT

In the sixth chapter of this book I took the liberty of mentioning several women within ministry from the eighteenth through twentieth centuries, and there are lots more beyond them. For this chapter's postscript, I'll go through a list with details about some of those women.

Clarissa Danforth (1792-1855)
Clarissa was the first woman ordained as a Free Will Baptist minister. Danforth was born in Weathersfield, Vermont in 1792. She heard Rev. John Colby preach in 1809 on his way to Ohio and gave her heart to The Lord. She was ordained in 1815 and became a traveling preacher throughout northern New England. After the passing of John Colby, she began preaching in Chepachet, Rhode Island and the surrounding areas in 1818

after taking over as pastor of the Chepachet Baptist Church. Clarissa spent most of her preaching days in Rhode Island and was instrumental leading the revival in Smithfield that sparked from the Greenville Baptist Church. She also preached at times in Massachusetts, New Hampshire and Vermont. She married Danford Richmond a Baptist minister from Pomfret, Connecticut in 1822 and they moved to New York where she didn't preach as much as previously. Clarissa died around 1855.

Helenor M. Davison (1823-1876)

Helenor found salvation in Christ at an early age. She was the caregiver of her seven siblings, she nursed her family who had typhoid fever, and worked in her uncle's sawmill as a girl. She was a preacher's daughter. As an adult, she was ordained as a deaconess and a minister within the Methodist Church. An objection was made to her credibility only a year after her ordination as a minister for worthiness as a minister because she was a woman. Helenor cofounded a church with her dad. Her gravestone reads: "Helenor M. dau. of Rev. John Alter & wife of T.H. Davisson, Died Oct. 9. 1876, Aged 53 yrs. 8 mos. & 10 dys. The first ordained female in the United States"

Amanda Berry Smith (1837-1915)

Amanda was born a slave in Maryland to and was able to buy her family's freedom. They moved to Pennsylvania and started a station in the Underground Railroad.

She joined the African Methodist Episcopal Church after becoming a Christian. She felt the call to preach in 1869. She became a popular speaker and had opportunities to speak from Tennessee all the way up to Maine. The people loved Amanda's beautiful singing voice and anointed sermons. In 1878, she became the first black woman international evangelist, traveling to England, Ireland, Scotland, India and several African countries for twelve years.

Abigail (Abbie) Ellsworth Danforth (1841-1923)

The Ohio Universalist Convention ordained Abbie in 1878. She served Universalist churches in Ohio, including churches in Kent, Peru, Flint, Huntington, Bryan, Margaretta, and Le Roy, and was active in the Ohio Women's Missionary Society. In 1902, she moved to Tacoma, Washington, and served as minister of the Universalist Society until 1904. She also became Vice President of the Washington Equal Suffrage Association.

Anna Howard Shaw (1847-1919)

The first woman ordained in the Methodist Protestant Church was Anna Howard Shaw. It was one of the earlier denominations that would combine forces with others to form The United Methodist Church. She was born in New-castle-upon-Tyne in 1847. When she was four, she and her family immigrated to the United States and settled in Lawrence, Massachusetts. When Anna was twelve years old, her father took up claim of three hundred and sixty acres of land in the wilderness of northern Michigan "and sent her mother and five young children to live there alone. Her mother had thought their new home would be like "an English farm" with "deep meadows, sunny skies and daisies," but was devastated upon their arrival to discover that it was actually a "forlorn and desolate" log cabin "in what was then a wilderness, 40 miles from a post office and 100 miles from a railroad. The family experienced all the hardship and danger of frontier life. Anna stepped up to the plate and decided she would take on many responsibilities to help her family during this time of hardship, helping her siblings fix up their home and supporting her mother in her time of shock and despair. Anna did many rigorous tasks such as digging a well, chopping wood for the big fireplace, and falling trees.

Anna blamed her father for her mother's emotional distress and thought it very irresponsible to cause such hardship to the family. Instead of doing much to help out around the homestead, her father gave much of his time to the abolition movement and other causes of that day.

As the years went by, the family's misfortune grew worse. During the Civil War, her sister Eleanor died giving birth, and her brother Tom was wounded. When Anna was fifteen, she became a schoolteacher and after her older brothers and father joined the war effort, she used her earnings to help support her family, but the money wasn't enough to float all of the expenses.

As Anna matured, she developed a strong desire to attend college. She abandoned her teaching job after the civil war and moved in with her married sister Mary in Big Rapids, Michigan. Even though she disliked it, she became a seamstress even though she would have preferred to do work like digging ditches.

Reverend Marianna Thompson was the first person that supported her pursuit of an education and inspired her preaching career. Thanks to Thompson's help, Anna entered Big Rapids High School where the preceptress, Lucy Foot, recognized Shaw's talents and drive. At the age of twenty-four, Shaw was invited by Dr. Peck, a man looking to ordain a woman in the Methodist ministry, to give her first sermon. Anna hesitated at first because her only previous experience had been "as a little girl preaching alone in the forest...to a congregation of listening trees. With encouragement from Lucy Foot, Dr. Peck, and her close friend, Clara Osborn, Anna agreed and gave her first sermon in Ashton, Michigan.

Anna experience a lot of negative attention about her preaching even though her first sermon was a success. Despite such continual opposition and isolation from so many, Anna chose to keep on preaching. She was "deeply moved" by Mary A. Livermore, a prominent lecturer who came to Big Rapids. Ms. Livermore gave her the following advice: "if you want to preach, go on and preach...No matter what people say, don't let them stop you!" In 1873, the Methodist Church "voted unanimously to grant her a local preacher's license."

In 1873, Anna entered Albion College, a Methodist school in Albion, Michigan. Since her family frowned upon her decided career path, they refused to provide any financial support. At that point, Shaw had been a licensed preacher for three years and earned her wages by giving lectures on temperance.

After Albion College, Anna attended Boston University School of Theology in 1876. She was the only woman in her class of forty-two men, and she always felt "the abysmal conviction that [she] was not really wanted there." This attitude was furthered by her difficulty supporting herself financially. Already running on a tight income, Shaw found it unfair that the "male licensed preachers were given free accommodations in the dormitory and their board cost each of them $1.25 while it cost her $2 to pay rent of a room outside." Additionally, she had trouble finding employment. Unlike in Albion where she was "practically the only licensed preacher available", at Boston University there were many preachers who she had to compete with. As she lost money to pay the rent, she struggled to feed herself and felt "cold, hunger, and lonel[y]." Now Shaw started to question whether the ministerial profession was meant for her. In the face of these hardships, Shaw continued on. In 1880, after she and Annie Oliver were refused ordination by the Methodist Episcopal Church, despite passing with the top exam score that year [3]; she achieved ordination in the Methodist Protestant Church.

Following her ordination, Shaw received an MD from Boston University in 1886. During her time in medical school, she became an outspoken advocate of political rights for women.

Maria Woodworth-Etter (1844-1924)
At thirteen years old, Woodworth-Etter converted to Christianity. She "heard the voice of Jesus calling me to go

out in the highways and hedges and gather in the lost sheep." Her denomination prohibited her from public ministry, so she found support in a local Quaker meeting.

In 1885, she began preaching and praying for the sick. Her healing meetings drew such crowds that she eventually purchased an 8,000-seat tent. She was pivotal in founding the Assemblies of God church in 1914, and in 1918 she founded what is today Lakeview Church in Indianapolis.

In 1916, Maria preached, "God is calling the Marys and Marthas today all over our land to work in various places in the vineyard of the Lord; God grant that they may respond and say, 'Lord, here am I. Send me.' … My dear sister in Christ, as you hear these words may the Spirit of God come upon you, and make you willing to do the work the Lord has assigned to you."

Clara Celestia Hale Babcock (1850-1925) was the first woman ordained in the Christian Church (Disciples of Christ), which was known as the Christian Church, at that time. She held pastorates in four churches, conducted numerous evangelistic meetings and personally baptized at least 1,500 people. Clara Celestia Hale was born on May 31, 1850 in Fitchville, Ohio. She married Israel Babcock in 1865.Formerly members of the Methodist Church, the Babcocks joined the Stone-Campbell Movement in 1880 at the Sterling Christian Church in Sterling, Illinois.

Clara was also active in local temperance movements and served as a leader in the Woman's Christian Temperance Union, becoming president of the Whiteside County union in Whiteside, Illinois in 1887. Following a speaking engagement that was likely on behalf of the WCTU at an Erie, Illinois church in 1888, [2][3] the congregation urged Babcock to be their minister.

She was ordained by Andrew Scott of the Sterling Christian Church in 1889. Babcock participated in twenty-eight annual revivals and served as a pastor at churches throughout Illinois, Iowa, and North Dakota. Prior to her death in 1924, Babcock served as a pastor in Savanna, Illinois.

Louisa Woosley (1862-1952) was impressed at the age of twelve to labor in the vineyard of the Lord, seeing the harvest was truly plenteous and the laborers few. When she married, she hoped her husband would become a preacher, but he was not inclined to do so. Her own call became stronger and stronger. She read through her Bible, marking every place a woman is mentioned. At the end of her study, she was "convinced of the fact that God, being no respecter of persons, had not overlooked the women, but that he had a great work for them to do."

In the absence of a pastor one Sunday, Woosley preached her first sermon. After that, her call became irrepressible. She was ordained in 1889 by the Nolin Presbytery, becoming the first woman ordained as minister in any Presbyterian denomination and the first woman ordained in any Reformed tradition in America.

For the next thirty years, her ordination was a source of great controversy within the Kentucky synod. She wrote a defense of women's ordination entitled, Shall

Women Preach? Her ministry was marked by courage and tenacity in the face of harsh discrimination.

Ella Niswonger (1865-1944) was the first woman ordained in the American United Brethren Church, which later merged with other denominations to form the American United Methodist Church, which has ordained women with full clergy rights and conference membership since 1956.

She was born April 5, 1865 in Montgomery County, Ohio. She had three brothers and seven sisters. Her father, Eli Niswonger, was of German descent and was born in Montgomery County, Ohio. Her mother Elizabeth (nee) Miller was born in Lancaster County, Pennsylvania.

Ella was converted on December 22, 1880, and joined the United Brethren Church on January 2, 1881. She graduated in the regular course of Union Biblical Seminary (now United Theological Seminary), Dayton, Ohio, on May 4, 1887, and was ordained by Bishop E. B. Kephart on September 11,1889 in the United Brethren Church. Ella was the first woman to serve as ministerial delegate to the General Conference held in Frederick, Maryland in 1901. She received a quarterly conference license in August 1887, and became a member of the Central Illinois Conference. Her work as pastor began the following month at Streator, Illinois. She served there continuously, except for a brief stint with the Kansas Conference, until 1940 when she retired on account of the illness of her sister.

Reverend Niswonger died in Springfield, Illinois on August 2, 1944 at age seventy-nine. Her funeral was

conducted at the First United Brethren Church in Springfield, and interment was in the Parish Cemetery at Arling-
ton, Ohio.

Lucy Farrow (1851-1911)

Farrow was born into slavery in Virginia, and was
the niece of prominent black abolitionist Frederick Dou-
glass. In 1905, she was the pastor of a Holiness church in
Houston, Texas, when Charles Parnham of Bethel Bible
College hired her as governess for his children. Farnham
left her church in the care of a friend named William
Seymour.

In 1906, Seymour asked Farrow to come to Los
Angeles to teach glossalia to the people he was praying
with for revival. Her arrival sparked what came to be
known as the Azusa Street Revival. Her touch filled people with the Holy Spirit, and her ministry demonstrated
healings and the power of prayer. From Azusa Street, her
ministry spread throughout the Southern United States
and to Liberia and West Africa.

Agnes White Diffee (1886-1970) became the
youngest revivalist in the country at the age of sixteen.
Despite being an effective evangelist, she once said, "I
tried to be excused from answering the call to the ministry because I was a woman. I would not have minded if
I had been a man, but to be called a 'woman preacher'
was more than I could bear."

In 1919, she was ordained as senior pastor of a
Nazarene church in Amity, Arkansas, and went on to pastor First Nazarene in Little Rock. In twenty years, her congregation grew from under 300 to over 1,000. Diffee pas-

tored for thirty-five years, and once said, "I urge young women to keep an ear turned to Heaven for the call of God to preach the gospel."

Aimee Semple McPherson (1890-1944) was already a widow at nineteen while serving as a missionary in China. She returned to America and married again, and was mother to two children at twenty-three when she was dying from appendicitis and heard God ask her, "Now will you go?" She understood she could choose ministry or eternity. She began her ministry as a traveling evangelist.

McPherson and her mother eventually settled in Los Angeles to establish a permanent ministry. McPherson's church, the Angelus Temple, attracted 40 million visitors within its first seven years

McPherson captured the attention of the media; she became one of the most widely photographed people at the time. A reporter once described McPherson's sermons: "Never did I hear such language from a human being. Without one moment's intermission, she would talk from an hour to an hour and a half, holding her audience spellbound." She would preach twenty-two sermons a week, and was the first preacher to use the radio to broadcast sermons. She is considered the first celebrity pastor.

Inspired by her Salvation Army roots, McPherson required every church member to be involved in charitable work. During the Great Depression, the Angelus Temple fed 1.5 million people, and was considered the most effective charitable organization at the time. She once said, "What is my task? To get the gospel around the world in the shortest possible time to every man and woman and boy and girl!"

Elisabeth Schmidt (1908-1986) embodied the fight for women pastors within the French Reformed Church. She was the daughter of a Member of Parliament and studied philosophy at the Sorbonne in Paris and then theology in Geneva. From 1935 to 1941 she was assistant with the Saint Croix Vallée Française parish in the Cévennes region and then in Sète until 1958. The parishioners themselves asked for her ordination.

Geneviève Jonte (1906-1983) was the daughter and granddaughter of the Montbéliard region pastors. She studied theology in Paris, then was an assistant with the Montbéliard parish in 1934, and was eventually ordained in 1937. She was the first pastor of the small Saint John temple the Peugeot family had paid for and built in the new workers' quarters – it was later demolished when the Peugeot Company needed the land.

Marieleine Hoffet (1905-1996) was a pastor's daughter who studied theology in Strasburg, Geneva and Edinburgh. She was a vicar with the Reformed Church of Alsace Lorraine and got married in 1931. She took an active part in the resistance movement and accepted in 1945 a position no one wished to take, namely chaplain in former collaborators' internment camps. She then turned to women's bible teaching. She fought against the rule forbidding married women to become pastors, which was suspended in 1968.

Margaret Ellen Towner (1925-Current) is an American religious leader who was the first woman to be ordained a minister of the Presbyterian Church of the U.S.A. (PCUSA), the northern branch of the American Presbyterian Church. She was born March 19, 1925, in Columbia, Missouri, to Milton Carsley Towner and Dorothy Marie (Schloeman) Towner. She majored in pre-medical studies at Carleton College, receiving her B.A. in 1948. Afterwards, she worked as a medical photographer for the Mayo Clinic. She left the clinic and enrolled at Syracuse University in New York to study Christian audiovisual education; around the same time, she began volunteering at local churches in Syracuse (First Presbyterian Church) and East Genesee.

In 1955, the PCUSA voted to begin ordaining women as ministers. The following year, on Oct. 24, 1956, Towner became the first woman ordained to the ministry by PCUSA, with her ordination taking place at Syracuse-Cayuga Presbytery in New York. (Nine years later, the church's southern branch, the Presbyterian Church in the U.S. (PCUS) would ordain its first woman minister, Rachel Henderlite.) Since there were a number of Presbyterian women preparing for ordination in the wake of the PCUSA vote, Towner was initially not sure whether she was actually the first to be ordained. Her ordination was covered by Life photographer Alfred Eisenstaedt, and photographs of Towner's ordination ceremony appeared in a five-page spread in the November 12, 1956, issue of the magazine.

After being ordained, Towner returned to her congregation in Pennsylvania, though she was never asked to conduct services or preach in that church; and she was also made assistant pastor of First Presbyterian Church in Syracuse. Afterwards, she served at congregations in Kalamazoo, Michigan (First Church, 1958–69); Indianapolis, Indiana (Northminster Presbyterian Church, 1970–72); and Milwaukee, Wisconsin (Kettle Moraine parish, 1973-1990). At first she worked mainly in Christian education and as an assistant or associate pastor, only later becoming a full pastor. It was not until her very last posting that she was paid equally with male pastors. She spent 17 years in Milwaukee, where she was one of three co-pastors in a parish with six churches.

In 1981, the year that PCUSA celebrated the 25th anniversary of women's ordination in the church, Towner was elected vice-moderator of the church's General Assembly. Among her activities that year was a trip to Korea to talk to Presbyterian congregations, as the Korean churches were then considering whether to ordain women. In 1990, at the end of her Milwaukee pastorate, she retired to Sarasota, Florida.

Even though the PCUSA was not yet ordaining women as ministers, change was in the air, and the pastor at First Presbyterian Church suggested that Towner should explore the ministry. The church offered her its Scattergood Fellowship to attend Union Theological Seminary in New York, where Towner undertook the three-year program leading to a Bachelor of Divinity degree, which she received in 1954. A decade later, in 1967, she received an M.A. in guidance and counseling from Western Michigan University. [citation needed]

After obtaining her B.D., Towner was commissioned a church worker. She became director of Christian education at Takoma Park Presbyterian Church in Maryland (1954-1955) and then at First Presbyterian Church in Allentown, Pennsylvania (1955–58).

In 1983, Towner was given the Distinguished Alumnus Award by Carleton College. In 1989, she was awarded an honorary doctorate of divinity by Carroll College. In 2006, the Milwaukee Presbytery established the Doctor Margaret E. Towner scholarship in her honor. A number of women who followed Towner in the Presbyterian ministry have credited her as their role model and mentor.

Addie Elizabeth Davis (1917-2005) became the first woman to be ordained to the gospel ministry by a Southern Baptist congregation – Watts Street Baptist Church in Durham, North Carolina. At the time of her ordination, Rev. Davis was a student of Southeastern Baptist Theological Seminary. Not all Baptists in the Durham area took kindly to Davis' ordination. She received dozens and dozens of letters spewing with vitriol. One of these letters urged Davis to "learn from her husband." Davis never married. One man from Richmond, Virginia demanded that Davis renounce her ordination. Another man called her "a child of the Devil."

Unable to find a pastoral position in a Southern Baptist church, Davis had to leave the South in order to practice the vocation given to her by God. Eventually, Davis was called to pastor First Baptist Church in Reads-boro, Vermont. According to David Stricklin, author of A Genealogy of Dissent, Davis' experience showed how people's attitudes are conditioned by what they observe. Davis "once noticed some children of the congregation she was serving in Vermont 'playing church.' When one of the little boys wanted to take his turn being the preacher, his older sister admonished him saying, 'You can't be the preacher; only women are preachers!' Such was not the attitude of most of the people from the region of her upbringing."

Baptist Women in Ministry established the Addie Davis Awards in 1995 to honor Addie Davis, the first Southern Baptist woman ordained to the gospel ministry. These awards are also a way for BWIM to give public recognition to gifted women seminarians. That year and in the years since, BWIM has requested nominations for the awards from Baptist seminaries, divinity schools, and houses of study. Each theological institution is asked to nominated two women students: one for the Addie Davis Awards for Excellence in Preaching and one for the Addie Davis Award for Outstanding Leadership in Pastoral Ministry.

Upon Addie Davis' death in 2005, Pam Durso remarked that "what made Addie Davis so remarkable was not her place in history as the first woman to be ordained by a Southern Baptist church; it was her humility, her compassion, and her warm spirit. She faithfully followed God's calling, serving three churches as pastor or co-pastor. Her focus in those churches was on caring for the people and being with them in times of crisis." Through-out her ministry, Davis often encouraged other women to "keep on dreaming and cherish the dream God has giv-en you!" However, the Southern Baptist Convention stopped ordaining women in 2000, although existing fe-male pastors are allowed to continue their jobs.

Rachel Henderlite (1905-1991) was an American religious leader who was the first woman to be ordained a pastor of the Presbyterian Church of the United States (PCUS), the southern branch of the Presbyterian Church in the United States of America. She held professorships at several American colleges and seminaries, wrote six books, and was active in various ecumenical efforts.

Rachel was born in Henderson, North Carolina, on December 30, 1905, one of three children of James Hen-ry Henderlite and Nelle (Crow) Henderlite. Her father was a Presbyterian pastor who advocated for a reunification of the southern and northern branches of the American church; Henderlite spent much time with him, and her religious views were shaped by his influence. She at-tended high school in Gastonia, North Carolina, and went on to study at Mary Baldwin College in Virginia for two years. She earned her B.A. in English from Agnes Scott College in Georgia (1928) after taking some time off due to tuberculosis. For a time after college, she taught high school English. In 1931, Henderlite moved to New York at attend the Biblical Seminary, graduating with an M.A. in Christian education (1936).

Henderlite took a post as dean and professor of Bible studies at Mississippi Synodical College, staying until 1938, when she moved on to a similar professorship at Montreat College in North Carolina. After three years, she left Montreat College to care for her father, who was in failing health. During this period she returned to teaching at local high schools. After her father's death in 1942, Henderlite enrolled at Yale University Divinity School to study Christian ethics under H. Richard Niebuhr. Yale would later (1947) award her a Ph.D. in Christian ethics.

In 1944, she accepted a professorship in applied Christianity and Christian nurture at the General Assembly's School for Lay Workers (ATS, later known as the Presbyterian School of Christian Education and today as the Union Presbyterian Seminary) in Richmond, Virginia. At the time, ATS was primarily a graduate school, and it taught many women who were training for positions (such as missionary work) that did not require ordination, as the American Presbyterian churches did not ordain women at that time. In addition to teaching standard courses on the Bible and Christian education, she inaugurated a series of courses on her specialty, Christian ethics. In 1966, she accepted a professorship in Christian education at Austin Presbyterian Theological Seminary in Texas. She retired from full-time teaching six years later.

Henderlite served on the PCUS's Board of Education (1957–59) in various capacities, including as a director of educational research and director of curriculum development. In these positions, she is credited with leading the development of what became known as "The Covenant Life Curriculum," the church's first curriculum to "deal seriously with social ethics from a Christian perspective". She also served as the only North American representative to a series of meetings sponsored by the World Alliance of Reformed Churches in the 1950s to advise on marriage theology and interfaith marriage.

Between 1966 and 1981, she was active in the Consultation on Church Union, a joint conference of 10 North American Christian denominations. In 1977, she became the first woman to serve as the group's president, a position she held for five years.

Henderlite served on the PCUS's Board of Education (1957–59) in various capacities, including as a director of educational research and director of curriculum development. In these positions, she is credited with leading the development of what became known as "The Covenant Life Curriculum," the church's first curriculum to "deal seriously with social ethics from a Christian perspective". [2] She also served as the only North American representative to a series of meetings sponsored by the World Alliance of Reformed Churches in the 1950s to advise on marriage theology and interfaith marriage.

Between 1966 and 1981, she was active in the Consultation on Church Union, a joint conference of 10 North American Christian denominations. In 1977, she became the first woman to serve as the group's president, a position she held for five years. Henderlite was honored with the Union Medal from Union Theological Seminary in 1983. In 1990, the Presbyterian School of Christian Education established a scholarship in her name. She died of a heart attack on November 6, 1991, in Austin, Texas. Her papers are held by the Presbyterian Historical Society in Philadelphia, Pennsylvania.

CHAPTER 7 POST SCRIPT

Both exegetically and historically, it's quite clear that Phoebe of the New Testament as well a very many other women were recognized as deaconesses within the church. They continued in this servant role through the Byzantine, later called Orthodox Church, while the Catholic Church in the fifth through eleventh centuries tried to suppress women from certain ministerial roles. Because of all of this it has become apparent to many that the Apostle Paul and the first century church understood a gender neutrality to the office of deacon, as that's what we see commended via Phoebe in scripture, and practiced. This has raised the question to some theologians, scholars, and archeologist whether the role of Overseer or Bishop was likewise an egalitarian role, whereas the verbiage applied is the same.

Within early Christendom, the feminine form of "presbyter" or elder occurs frequently, though it is often translated simply as "old woman." Some scholars assert at times the term certainly refers to women who were part of the clergy. The Cappadocian father, Basil, uses presbytera apparently in the sense of a woman who is head of a religious community. Also applied to women is the term presbutis, "older woman" or "eldress." The old woman who instructed Hermas is called presbytis. It occurs not only in Titus 2:3, but most markedly in Canon 11 of Laodicea, which forbade the appointment of presbytides (eldresses) or of female presidents (prokathemenai).

The masculine form, prokathemenos, indicated the presbyter or bishop who presided over the communion service. Dionysius of Alexandria, who died in 264 A.D., described a martyr as "the most holy eldress Mercuria" and another as "a most remarkable virgin eldress Apollonia." A variant reading of the apocryphal Martyrdom of Matthew, a 4th- or 5th-century document, tells how Matthew ordained a king as priest and his wife as presbytis, "eldress." Epiphanius and Theodoret vehemently repudiated any priestly function accruing to the "presbytides."

The 5th century image of a woman named Cerula, found in the catacomb of San Gennaro, Naples, shows her surrounded by open, flaming Gospel books, which are thought to be symbolic of the role of a bishop. The wall paintings, hidden for 1,000 years, were rediscovered in 1971 and recently restored. Cerula was painted in the late 5th or early 6th century and is depicted in the praying position, hands raised, with the "chi-rho" symbol of Christ over her head. Crucially, she is surrounded by open volumes of all four gospels, suggesting that she had real influence and responsibility. Dr. Ally Kateusz, an expert in early Christian art, told the programme: "That's really extraordinary, because bishops were associated with the gospels.

"Bishops, and bishops only, had open gospel books placed over their heads during their ordination ritual. "The flames of the holy spirit would come out of the gospels and inspire the bishops in their preaching."

Mosaic of Bishop Theodora (820 AD) in a side chapel in St. Praxedis Church, Rome.

Next to Theodora is St. Praxedes, then the Virgin Mary, and St. Pudentiana. Praxedes and Pudentiana were 2nd century sisters who reportedly built a font in their house and began baptizing pagans. The two were second century martyrs for Christ and this Church was named after Praxedes. "Bishop Theodora" is the bishop of the Church of St. Praxedis in 820 A.D. The square halo indicates that she was still alive when the mosaic was made. The style of her head covering signifies that she was not married. The title "EPISCOPA" (Greek for Bishop) over Bishop Theodora's head. (The "r a" at the end of Theodora has been purposefully damaged.) But she also wears the episcopal cross that signifies her role as a bishop.

There is some argument about the epigraphical evidence for who Bishop Theodora is. The Latin reads thus:

"Et in ipso ingressu basilicae manu dextra ubi utique benignissimae suae genitricis scilicet domnae Theodorae Episcopae corpus quiescit condidit iam dictus praesul corpora venerabilium haec Zenonis et aliorum quorum."

Some scholars have translated it thus: "And at the entrance of the basilica on the right hand side where the body of his most kind mother lady Bishop Theodora rests, the aforementioned bishop (Pope Paschal I) interred the bodies of the venerable Zeno and others…"

Others have translated the Latin this way:
"And at the very entrance of the basilica on the right side where his mother (The Virgin Mary), (for whom we should give thanks) is, where the body of Lady

Theodore Bishop rests, this venerable bishop (Pope Paschal I) interred the bodies of venerable Zeno and others."

Within the Synod and Canon XI of Laodicea there is much reference to debate and thoughts concerning women within the roles of Bishops/Elders and Deaconesses. In short, they only substantiate that women were in fact both Deaconesses and Elders within the church body. However, the writers of "Canon XI of Laodicea" also determine that these female eldresses and deaconess responsibilities were to the women of the early church. They also surmise that the Apostle Paul's qualification of seventy years old was entwined with a woman's applicability to be an eldress.

EPILOGUE POST SCRIPT

Within a worldview based purely on naturalism, neither mankind nor womankind have any value. From that evolutionary stance, we are nothing more than a byproduct of time plus chance plus matter. Within Gnosticism it is the man (Adam) not the woman who is given the spark of God via Sophia, thus devaluing womankind. There are multiple examples of this gross misogyny throughout many Gnostic texts. In correctly understanding the Bible we find this is not the case. I certainly hope this book has helped shine a light in the darkness for you the reader.

About the Author

Benjamin Lee Blankenship was born in Toledo, Ohio. When he was fourteen years old, his family then moved to the small East Tennessee town of Rockwood. Benjamin gave his heart to The Lord at a very early age. He heard the voice of God call him to preach at the tender age of seven. He then asked his mother what it took to be a preacher. She told him that it would take long hours of study and hard work. Due to fear, he would not profess his calling until age 14. After wrestling with feelings of inadequacy, he preached his first sermon a week before his 18th birthday.

The following year, Ben's Uncle Terry Smith was on his death bed. Terry was a very talented songwriter, singer and musician who had been with the popular 1960's group "The Mods" who won " The Battle of the Bands" in 1966. Ben fervently prayed to receive his uncle's gift of songwriting to be bestowed upon him. Upon his uncle's passing, Ben quickly discovered that The Lord had answered his prayer. He began writing songs under the anointing of The Holy Ghost. It was during that time that he felt a burden for groups to pick up his songs to be put out to radio. Due to being an unknown in the music industry, his dream wouldn't come to pass during that time. Because of rejection and unresponsiveness, Ben decided to form his own group so his music could be heard. His first group was called" No Doubts" which had a run of about 2 years. Shortly thereafter he formed "BEN*JAM" which produced multiple albums and sent several songs to radio. In 2018, Ben decided to put BEN*JAM in a semi retirement state due to the demands of pastoring at Benchmark Church. Ben has written well over 100 songs and several have been recorded by artists such as: Bob Smallwood and Caleb Howard with recording plans being made by Steve Warren, Dennise Nichole Dittman-Cook, Bryan James Hatton and others.

Benjamin's preaching ministry began with evangelizing in churches and nursing homes. This soon led to the pastorship of his first church in a small storefront in Rockwood, Tennessee. In January 2015, Ben began pastoring his second church, Benchmark Church where he is currently the pastor. During the spring of 2019, Ben felt inspired to do a " By Request Series" at church for Friday night services which led to the study of women in ministry. Upon completing many hours of Biblical research and scholarly material, Ben felt compelled to write this book due to the suppression and oppression of women in ministry have and are currently experiencing.